TORCH BIBLE COMMENTARIES

General Editors

John Marsh and Alan Richardson

THE EPISTLE TO
THE ROMANS

A. M. HUNTER

SCM PRESS LTD
BLOOMSBURY STREET LONDON

334 01403 4

First published 1955
Second impression 1957
Third impression 1961
Fourth impression 1968
Fifth impression 1973
Sixth impression 1975

© SCM Press Ltd 1955

Printed in Great Britain by
Fletcher & Son Ltd, Norwich

CONTENTS

the Old Testament, as so many 'Jewish old clothes'. The
very suggestion would have been anathema to the apostolic
preachers who found in the Old Testament the one indis-
pensable key to the New: for them these 'Jewish old
clothes' were the swaddling-bands of the Saviour of the
world. It was the first plank in their platform that in Christ
God's promises to ancient Israel through 'his servants the
prophets' had come true.

3. Second, the good news concerns God's SON. In Jewish
circles of Paul's time, 'Son of God' could be another name
for the Messiah. But when Paul calls Jesus God's Son,
especially when he adds the clarifying word OWN (as he does
in Rom. 8.3,32), he claims more than Messiahship for him:
the phrase describes Jesus as a being who stands in a unique
filial relation to the almighty Father, a being at once human
and divine. In respect of his human nature—ACCORDING TO
THE FLESH—Jesus was a descendant of David, and therefore
a properly accredited Messiah. THERE SHALL COME FORTH
A ROOT OUT OF THE STEM OF JESSE ran the prophecy (Isa.
11.1).[1] In respect of his divine nature—ACCORDING TO THE
SPIRIT OF HOLINESS—he has been DECLARED TO BE THE SON
OF GOD WITH POWER by the Resurrection. Son of God he
had been before, in humiliation, during his ministry. By
God's 'mighty act' (*dynamis*: lit. 'power') on the first
Easter day he has been signally disclosed for what he really
was—and is.

4-5. Jesus Christ our Lord

The early Christian *credo* in brief. JESUS signifies the
remembered person; CHRIST the Saviour promised to Israel;
OUR LORD the divine being with whom Christians commune
in worship and sacrament. And this Lord is the mediator
of their GRACE AND APOSTLESHIP. GRACE—the free, un-

[1] cf. Isa. 9.6; Jer. 23.5.

merited favour of God to sinners—is the possession of all
Christians, as APOSTLESHIP describes Paul's special com-
missioning as Christ's envoy. The purpose of these divine
gifts was to bring the Gentiles to THE OBEDIENCE OF FAITH—
a phrase which may mean either 'the obedience which consists in faith' or 'the obedience which springs from faith'.

7. To all that are in Rome

At last Paul reaches the recipients of the letter—the
'addressees'. The phrasing suggests they are mostly Gentiles.
Like him, they are objects of God's love and are CALLED TO
BE SAINTS. Saints, in the New Testament, does not mean
people who (to use academic terms) have already achieved
'alpha plus' in the life of holiness (though that is their
ultimate goal); it means, as Luther saw, 'justified sinners'
—people who having heard God's call and accepted his forgiveness in Christ, are 'right' with God.

Paul wishes them GRACE AND PEACE FROM GOD OUR FATHER
AND THE LORD JESUS CHRIST. (Note how this born-and-bred
monotheist can set Jesus unequivocally on that side of reality
which we call divine; and that too within thirty years of the
Crucifixion.) The ordinary greeting in a Greek letter,
chairein (lit. 'rejoice'), Paul turns into *charis*, 'grace', with
all its Christian overtones. PEACE (*shālôm*) was the normal
Jewish greeting, but on Paul's lips it must mean that inner
serenity which belongs to those who, through Christ, have
made their peace with God.

4. Declared to be

The Greek *horisthentos* might also be translated 'in-
stalled', suggesting an Adoptionist Christology, unlike Paul's,
which is Incarnationist. SPIRIT OF HOLINESS. Again, the
Greek (*pneuma hagiōsynēs*) might be differently interpreted.
'Spirit of holiness' may be a Hebrew way of saying 'Holy
Spirit'.

8-17. THANKSGIVING AND PERSONAL INTRODUCTION

It was Paul's normal practice to follow the address with a thanksgiving. Here the thanksgiving quickly passes over into a personal explanation.

Paul gives thanks to God, through Christ the mediator, for the Church in Rome whose Christian witness (he says with pardonable hyperbole) is known the world over. He had often designed to visit the capital (Cf. Acts 19.21, I MUST ALSO SEE ROME). Not unwarrantably, he felt he could confer some SPIRITUAL GIFT on the Roman Christians. (If he means some of his insights into the gospel, we may judge that he imparted much of his gift in this letter.) Tactfully, he corrects any suggestion that the giving will be all his—his visit should spiritually invigorate both parties. What had prevented it hitherto was doubtless the pressure of evangelistic work elsewhere (see 15.22). But a harvest of souls in Rome, the hub of the great heathen world, was an understandable ambition for the Apostle to the Gentiles. The bearer of a universal message, he is ' under obligation '—by his divine call—to serve all men, irrespective of their language or culture. Hence his eagerness to preach in Rome. The gospel of a crucified carpenter in the streets of Imperial Rome—is not the idea so incongruous as to make one ashamed at the prospect? No, he is not ashamed, for the gospel is a divine POWER—God works in it—for saving sinners, and there are sinners enough in Rome, God knows. Such salvation the gospel announces—*and conveys*; and it is available for every man with faith, everyone ready to let the POWER have its way with him, be he Jew or Greek.

Such is the general drift of this passage, but there are some points in it that demand elucidation.

14. To Greeks and to Barbarians

To civilized and to uncivilized, educated and uneducated.

The ability to speak Greek was in those days the hall-mark
of the civilized man. Foreigners who could not speak Greek
were called 'barbarians', 'stammerers', from the unfamiliar
sound of their tongue.

16. It is the power of God

Paul calls the gospel God's *dynamis*, the word used elsewhere in the New Testament for a miracle or mighty work.
Of course, the gospel is about God's mighty work in Christ,
is the proclamation of a dynamic event. But here he thinks
of the gospel message as being itself a part of the continuing
dynamic event. 'Just as God used the life, death and resurrection of Jesus, so also, if in a subordinate way, he is using
the preaching of that life, death and resurrection as a
medium of his power.'[1]

To the Jew first and also to the Greek

Why THE JEW FIRST? The answer is: because of the
special position Israel had as as the historic People of God.
'The children first'. said Jesus (Mark 7.27). And as a
matter of plain historic fact, the gospel had been preached
first to the Jews.

17. A very important verse. What does Paul mean when
he says that THEREIN (i.e. in the gospel) A (or 'the')
RIGHTEOUSNESS OF GOD IS REVEALED?

To us THE RIGHTEOUSNESS OF GOD suggests a divine
attribute; to Paul, almost certainly, it suggested a divine
activity: the righteous God in action. It is a dynamic, not
a static phrase; and the clue to its meaning is in the Septua-
gint (or Greek version of the Old Testament) where again
and again—especially in the Psalms and Deutero-Isaiah—
dikaiosynē, rendering the Hebrew *tsedaqah*, means 'God
vindicating', 'God putting things right' for his oppressed

---

[1] John Knox, *The Interpreter's Bible*, 9, 391.

people, and righteousness becomes a synonym for 'salvation'. Thus Ps. 98.2:

'THE LORD HATH MADE KNOWN HIS SALVATION,
   HIS RIGHTEOUSNESS HATH HE OPENLY SHOWN IN THE
      SIGHT OF THE NATIONS.'

So we may define THE RIGHTEOUSNESS OF GOD as the activity in which he saves his people by rescuing them from their oppressors and delivering them from their sin.

Now for such divine vindication—for a day when God would decisively redress all wrong and put things right— prophet and psalmist yearned in the centuries before Christ's coming. It was the living heart of the messianic hope.

With this brief background we may now understand Paul when he says that in the gospel 'the righteousness of God is being revealed'. He is thinking of the divine activity by which God saves men in Jesus Christ crucified and risen. It is his way of saying that in the life, death and resurrection of Jesus the Kingdom (or sovereignty) of God has arrived. Furthermore, this act of God makes possible for man a new relationship with God. If God is putting things right for sinners in Christ, then the sinner who puts his faith in Christ, is accepted by God for Christ's sake. He is *justified*, that is, 'declared (or set) right' with God. And this means not only pardon for his past sins but also the gift of a new status or standing with God. But of all this Paul will have more to say later in his letter.

BY FAITH UNTO FAITH means that, on man's side, salvation is completely a matter of faith from start to finish. Cf. II Cor. 2.16. What then does Paul mean by faith?

The word carries various shades of meaning in Paul's letters ('faithfulness', confidence in God's promises, conviction of the unseen, etc.), but the peculiarly Pauline meaning is utter trust—trust with a strong element of obedience in it. The man who, for Paul, supremely exemplifies faith in the Old Testament is Abraham who, when God spoke to him, took God at his word and obeyed. Faith, for Paul,

means taking God at his word in Christ. It is the complete
response of the soul to the good news of God embodied in
Christ. Such faith is directed not to a proposition but to a
person—sometimes God, oftener Christ, the living Christ
with the virtue of his atoning death in him. It is not only
an act but an attitude—the attitude of a whole life (Gal.
2.20); and where it is true faith, it is a creative ethical force:
faith 'works through "love"', and a faith which does not
so express itself is a sham (I Cor. 13.2). Thus, faith is as
truly the whole of Christianity subjectively, as Christ is the
whole of it objectively.

The righteous shall live by faith

Paul clinches his point with this quotation from Hab. 2.4.
Habakkuk meant that in his troubles the righteous man
would 'come through' in virtue of his faithfulness, or
fidelity; Paul (as the RSV and Nygren insist) means that
'he who-by-faith is righteous shall live', i.e. be saved.
(Chapters 1-4 of this letter, in which the word faith occurs
no less than twenty-five times, simply expand the words 'he
who by faith is righteous', as chapters 5-8 explicate 'shall
live').

THE SIN OF MAN
1.18–3.20

Now begins the first main section of the letter. Before
he prescribes the divine remedy, Paul, like a wise physician,
diagnoses the disease. The righteousness of God is needed
because of the unrighteousness of men. First, he indicts the
Gentiles for their sin (1.18-32), then the Jews (2.1-29), and
finally he declares that all men alike are sinners in God's
sight (3.1-20).

18-32. THE GREAT INDICTMENT (1) THE SIN OF
THE GENTILES
Apart from the gospel, Paul says, the world is lost. Look

out on the vast pagan world, and what you will see is the UNGODLINESS AND UNRIGHTEOUSNESS OF MEN against which God is openly manifesting his holy displeasure. So we paraphrase Paul's phrase THE WRATH OF GOD. 'I jest cain't stand sin', God is made to say in the negro play *Green Pastures*. That too is how Paul thinks of God. But can we? Is not THE WRATH OF GOD an outmoded theological fiction? Some exegetes, noting that Paul never says explicitly that 'God is angry with men', interpret the phrase in terms of an impersonal retribution—the inevitable process of cause and effect in a moral world, not to be too closely connected with God. But the Bible does not so deper-sonalize the idea. The prophets do not scruple to say that God is angry with men. Jesus himself, for all his stress on the divine goodness, is very emphatic that God cannot palter with sin but must react against it. And Paul speaks, at least three times, unequivocally of 'the wrath of God'.

The truth is that we dislike the phrase because we have sentimentalized our conception of God in a quite un-biblical way. Wrath—the strong and continuous reaction of the holy God against evil in every shape and form—a wrath operative now and not only at the Last Judgment, is an essential part of any truly biblical idea of God. Nor should we who have lived through the first half of the twentieth century boggle at it. 'Any age,' says Cragg,[1] 'which has seen the pomp of insolent evil overthrown, and has watched the fearful retribution which wrong-doing can bring on those who practice it should be ready to reconsider the significance of the wrath of God.' But if we do so, we must remember two things. First, God's wrath is not to be thought of in terms of sinful man's—as vindictive rage or the emotional reaction of an irritated self-concern. Rather, if we use human analogies, we should think of the 'righteous indigna-

---

[1] *The Interpreter's Bible*, 9, 397.

tion' a good man feels in the presence of stark evil—and
multiply it by infinity. Secondly, God's wrath is not incom-
patible with his love. (The opposite of love is hate.) We
should rather conceive God's wrath as the obverse of his
love—'the adverse wind', the antagonism of his holy love
to all that is evil.

The pagan world, Paul proceeds (v. 19), deserves God's
wrath because it has deliberately refused that knowledge of
himself which God has given them in his created works, and
has fallen into idolatry. Clearly Paul is thinking of what
we call nowadays 'a General Revelation' of God independ-
ent of the Special Revelation to the Jews. The creation
testifies to the Creator's power and deity; and man, looking
through nature up to nature's God, ought instinctively to
fall on his knees and worship. (It is a question whether
Paul is quite fair in outrightly condemning the heathen for
their failure to find God's revelation of himself in nature.
Sometimes the testimony of nature is not so clear and plain
as Paul maintains. There is some excuse for polytheists and
animists.)

Refusing this 'General Revelation', the Gentiles have
resorted to futile speculations which produce spiritual darkness and, in the end, idolatry. Apostasy from the true God
brings with it not only wrong worship but (its corollary)
wrong behaviour. The consequent sins of the Gentiles Paul
seems to divide up into two classes, (1) sins against nature,
like homosexuality (24-27), and (2) sins against society
(28-32). Or we may call them sensual sins and anti-social
sins—the latter, in Paul's opinion, being the fruits of A
REPROBATE MIND, i.e. a mind in which the moral distinctions
between right and wrong are blurred, and so rejected by
God. We have spoken as if these Gentile idolaters simply
relapsed into these fearful sins. Paul puts it more personally: GOD GAVE THEM UP, he says thrice over. Their
relapse into wickedness was God's punishment of them: it
is as if God, having held his protecting hand over them, had

suddenly withdrawn it, and let them take what they deserved.

These verses make grim reading. Is it not possible that Paul has put too much lamp-black into his picture of the Gentile world? We may recognize that Paul is writing as a prophet and not with the exactitude of a social historian. We must also remember that in the next chapter he will admit the existence of good pagans. But before we criticize the apostle, we should notice two things: (1) Most of the idolatry he mentions in v. 23 existed in Egypt in his day. (2) Juvenal's *Satires* abundantly testify to the moral rottenness of contemporary Roman society, as Suetonius's *Lives of the Emperors* show how rampant were the sins of the flesh in the highest circles. (Of Julius Caesar, commonly accounted one of the greatest men of all time, he reports this: 'He was every woman's man and every man's woman.' Tiberius and Nero were even worse.)

The root-cause of this demoralization Paul finds in the worship of false gods. The ignoring of the true God is the first fatal step that ends in this slough. Lose God, and you lose every atom of self-respect. (Lest we grow too superior, let us remember that the worship of the machine or of the State is as much idolatry as bowing down before 'sticks and stones'.)

Is Paul right in all this? Of course he is not here making a scientific contribution to comparative religion. What he is asserting is that religion and morality in the great scale hang together, and in the long run a man's, or a people's, morality is determined by what he worships. Who will dare to say that he is wrong? Is it only coincidence that in our day when so many people have slipped their spiritual moorings we are witnessing a widespread collapse of moral standards?

18. Hold down the truth

suggests a man holding down some living thing in a poisonous atmosphere till he stifles it.

C

23. For the likeness of an image of:
   'into images resembling.'

25. The truth of God: God in his truth.
   A lie: abstract for concrete.   Paul means the idol.

28. Things which are not fitting
   'Improper conduct': a Stoic phrase covering the whole
range of anti-social offences.

32. Consent with them
   The darkest stroke in the picture.   The public conscience
is dead.   Not only sinning themselves, they take cynical
delight in the wrong-doing of others.

II

*' But you, my Jewish friend, are no better. You condemn
sins like these, yet you do them yourself. God's patience is
not something to be presumed on—it is meant to make you
repent. Make no mistake: God will judge men quite im-
partially, according to the good or the evil they have done.
The standard for the Jew will be the law of Moses; for the
Gentile, that unwritten law of God which he has in his
conscience.*

*You may pride yourself on possessing a special revelation
of God in the written law, but all the time your behaviour
shows you no whit better than the Gentiles. And if you
try to shelter behind circumcision as some kind of divine
protective mark, remember that this avails only if it goes
along with inner obedience to God's will.'*

1-16. THE GREAT INDICTMENT (2) THE SIN OF THE JEWS

Here begins the indictment of the Jew, couched in the
apostrophe-cum-question style which the Stoic preachers
had popularized.

We are to imagine a Jew listening self-righteously to Paul's
denunciation of Gentile guilt. Paul rounds abruptly on him.
He, the Jew, is no less guilty. He is well aware that God
punishes such people. Then let him not suppose that *he* will
escape. God's forbearance has one purpose—to give him
the chance to mend his ways. Instead, he impenitently goes
on sinning and incurring God's displeasure. There is a
Judgment coming—one based on works—and on that day
God will have no favourites. All—Gentiles and Jews alike
—will be judged by their obedience to God's will as they

knew it; and doers, not mere hearers, will come safely through.

Three points call for special comment. To begin with, the thoughts Paul ascribes to the Jew in the opening verses are no mere airy inventions. Many Jews thought like this; for example, the man who wrote The Wisdom of Solomon. For the Gentile he expected God's judgment, while confident of immunity for himself. FOR EVEN IF WE SIN, he said, WE ARE THINE, KNOWING THY DOMINION (15.2). WHILE THEREFORE THOU DOST CHASTEN US, THOU SCOURGEST OUR ENEMIES TEN THOUSAND TIMES MORE (12.22). It is a frame of mind not unknown in Christian history.

Secondly, Paul says (vv. 6ff.) that a man's destiny on Judgment Day will depend not on whether he has known God's will but on whether he has done it. It will be a judgment according to works. Our first reaction is, 'How very unpauline! Does not Paul teach that a man is justified here and now by God's grace, on the score of his faith, and need not fear a last judgment based on works?' The seeming contradiction has led some to regard this passage as an accommodation to Jewish teaching. But Paul is not really inconsistent. Justification by faith does not mean a moral 'stand-still' for the Christian, so that God no longer expects good works from him. On the contrary, God expects the new life which justification initiates to express itself in good works—or, if you like, 'fruits of the Spirit'—and the prospect of a final reckoning should keep the Christian alertly mindful of the fact.

Thirdly, a Stoic of Paul's day would have approved the doctrine of the natural law in vv. 14-15. With the Greek moralists from Aristotle to the Stoics, Paul holds that the natural man has an instinctive sense of right and wrong, a *lex naturae*, as the Stoics called it. When a pagan instinctively does what the law requires, e.g. honours his parents or condemns adultery, even though he has never heard of the fifth or seventh commandments, he is obeying God's will and is A LAW UNTO HIMSELF. This inner law is not, in Paul's view, a different law, but only a less complete revelation of God's will than the law of Moses. Thus, the Gentile's obedience (or disobedience) to this natural law is on all fours with the Jew's obedience (or disobedience) to the law of Moses.

2. The remark of the imaginary Jewish interlocutor.

6. Ps. 62.12.

7. Before ETERNAL LIFE, i.e. full and final salvation, supply the words 'he will give'.

9. The Jew first:
    as a member of the elect people. YOU ONLY HAVE I KNOWN OF ALL THE FAMILIES OF THE EARTH, THEREFORE I WILL PUNISH YOU FOR ALL YOUR INIQUITIES (Amos 3.2).

12. Sinned without law. Gentiles.

Sinned under law. Jews.

13. Shall be justified
    Acquitted at Judgment Day. This verse (which St. James might have written) is not completed till v. 16: THE DOERS OF THE LAW SHALL BE JUSTIFIED . . . IN THE DAY WHEN GOD SHALL JUDGE, etc. Vv. 14-15 form a parenthesis.

2.17-19. THE INDICTMENT OF THE JEW CONTINUED
    Now begins, in real earnest, Paul's ' Thou art the man ! ' Threatened with God's wrath, the Jew imagines he can shelter behind two ' shields '—the law (17-24) and circumcision (25-29). Paul quickly disillusions him.
    The Jew he depicts must be a Pharisee—the kind of man Paul was before his conversion. He is proud of the unique

privilege he enjoys in the written revelation of God's will.
the law—the 'Word Incartulate',[1] so to say—which qualifies
him to be the teacher of divine truth to the benighted
heathen. But, says Paul, what a gulf yawns between his
privilege and his practice! For all his boasted 'light', the
Jew breaks the most elementary commandments of the law
—he steals, commits adultery, robs temples, just like 'any
lesser breed without the law'. Such treatment of the law
by a Jew can only bring discredit on the God he worships.
The pagan will inevitably—and sardonically—comment,
'What sort of a deity can he be whose Chosen People treat
his law like this!'

Theft, adultery, temple robbery—the charges Paul levels
against the Judaism of his day are serious. Are they true?
We may say that, if they were false, Paul would have
stultified his whole case. 'Nothing so recoils upon a debater
as accusations which are proved to be false.' But (though
there were undoubtedly many good Pharisees) in fact the
laments of contemporary rabbis, such as Johanan Ben
Zakkai, over the sin and corruption of their people, are
evidence enough that Paul was not making irresponsible
accusations. On the other hand (let us add), Christians
whose evil lives belie their high professions, no less dis-
honour the God and Father of our Lord Jesus Christ.

At this point (v. 25) we are to suppose the Jew taking
refuge behind his second shield—circumcision. Has not
the Jew a visible mark on his body showing that he is a
member of the Chosen Race and therefore a divine favourite? Has this historic mark no value? Of course it has value
for the Jew, Paul replies, but only if it is accompanied by a
corresponding inner obedience. What worth is the mark if
the people break the Covenant's law which it symbolizes?
In that case, the circumcised man might just as well have no
holy mark. Indeed, a pagan who has never heard of Moses,
but lives as the law requires, will condemn the Jew who, for

[1] The phrase is A. C. Craig's.

all his circumcision and written code, breaks the law. (See Matt. 12.41, Jesus said much the same about the Gentiles of Nineveh.) No, the whole point of being circumcised is obedience. No external mark can ever be a substitute for that, for though man may look on the outward appearance, God looks on the heart.

A good pagan, according to Paul, is better than a bad Jew. If the Jew who breaks the law, ceases to be a son of Abraham, the Gentile who observes it, though he has no mark on his body, is to all intents and purposes a true Israelite. In Jewish ears this must have sounded monstrous. Paul does not of course say that the pagan has no need of God's grace (all are sinners alike); but he does say that some Gentiles by their moral performance put the Jews to shame. Here again, we Christians may learn from Paul's strictures on the Jews. For 'circumcised' let us read 'churchman', and for 'uncircumcised', 'non-churchgoer' or even 'non-Christian'. Are we not all painfully aware that some non-Christians (Gandhi, for example) show more of the spirit of Christ in their lives than many professing churchmen?

17. Gloriest in God
viz. as the God of the Chosen Race.

18. Approvest the things that are excellent
Moffatt paraphrases this as 'with a sense of what is vital in religion'. The Greek might also mean: 'know the difference between right and wrong'.

Being instructed out of the law
In the synagogue, every sabbath. Cf. Acts 15.21.

19f. Guide of the blind; light of them that are in darkness; corrector of the foolish
may have been (as Althaus suggests) phrases used by the 'Foreign Mission Committee' of Pharisaic Judaism.

Form: ' outline '.

22. Rob temples:
Acts 19.37.

24. Isa. 52.5 in the LXX, the version Paul normally quotes.

26. Uncircumcision
Abstract for concrete. ' The Gentile '.

28. Circumcision should be spiritual as well as physical: a thought often found in the prophets—see Deut. 10.16 and Jer. 4.4.

Whose praise
A play on words. The word ' Jew '—descendant of Judah —means ' praise ' (Gen. 29.35). And such a Jew has his ' praise ' not from man but from God.

III

'The Jew may demur: "Is then a member of the Chosen People without any advantages?" No, he has many—e.g. the divine promises. "But has not Jewish unbelief nullified these promises?" No man's unbelief cannot make God break his plighted word. "Well, but if our sins call forth God's grace, is it not unfair of him to punish us?" No, the Judge of the world must do right, and people who argue that way deserve to be judged.

"Are the Jews any better off than the Gentiles?" No, the scripture convicts both equally as sinners. No man can get right with God by works of law. What the law does is to show us up as sinners.

But now a new era begins. God has openly begun to put things right for sinners, and his method, though in line with the old revelation, has no connexion with legal religion. It is a salvation based on faith in Christ, and open to everyone who has faith in him. (We are all sinners, remember.) God of his free grace sets us right with himself. The means is the deliverance wrought in the crucified Christ, whom God designed to be a means of forgiveness for the sinner with faith. Though in former times God forbearingly passed over sins, he now shows his will to judge sin and save sinners.

What follows? This, first: all "swanking" about earning one's own salvation is ruled out; and this, second: Jew and Gentile are on the same footing, since there is but one God and faith is the sole way of getting right with him.

Someone may object that this "system" undermines the old revelation. Nonsense! It confirms its deepest principles.'

41

1-8. THREE JEWISH OBJECTIONS

Before rounding off his proof of the universality of sin, Paul stops to dispose of three Jewish objections. To begin with, if (as Paul has argued) every difference between Jew and Gentile vanishes, are we to conclude that membership of the Chosen People carries no advantage with it? (Logically, Paul should have answered 'Yes, none'. But we may sympathize with him if we put the issue in modern terms: for Jew and Gentile substitute 'the Church' and 'the world'. Are we to say that there is no advantage in being a baptized Christian?) Paul rejects the suggestion. The Jew has many advantages: for example, the divine promises—but he stops short, faced with a second objection (v. 3). It is obvious that some Jews by their unbelief are forfeiting the promises. Will their unfaithfulness nullify God's faithfulness? No, answers Paul, whatever men do, God must keep his word. (He clinches his point with Ps. 51.4 in the LXX version.)

But, next (v. 5), a fresh objection appears. 'If,' says the Jewish heckler, 'our wickedness serves to show the righteousness of God, is it not unfair of God to inflict his wrath upon us?' No, replies Paul, this inference must be wrong, for we all know the supreme Judge must do right. This same objection the Jew now restates from man's side (v. 7): 'If, through my falseness, God's truthfulness appears gloriously, why am I condemned as a sinner? If our sin contributes to God's glory, should we not go on sinning that God may be magnified the more?' This, comments Paul, is just how some people mischievously pervert my teaching about God's grace. Later (in chapter 6) he will face up to this objection in earnest. Meantime he repels it with contempt. People, he says, who argue like this deserve all that is coming to them.

2. The oracles (*logia*) of God
The Old Testament scriptures, especially as containing the Messianic promises.

5. I speak after the manner of men
Paul apologizes for speaking of God as if he were a man.

9-20. THE UNIVERSALITY OF SIN
To complete his proof of the universality of sin, Paul forges a chain of six quotations from the Psalms and Isaiah (Ps. 14.1-3, 5.9, 140.3, 10.7, Isa. 59.7-8 and Ps. 36.1) as if to say, ' My charge is confirmed by the words of God himself '. The quotations, made without regard to the context, build up into a grim declaration of man's moral bankruptcy and guilt before God. Then (v. 19), as if to prevent the Jew saying, ' Oh, yes, but these words apply to the Gentiles ', he rivets them squarely on the people of the law. (THE LAW here means the whole Old Testament. Cf. I Cor. 14.21). Doing the law will never put a man right with God; for what the law does is to show us that we are sinners. Denney has well paraphrased v. 20a : ' Under no system of statutes, the Mosaic or any other, will flesh ever succeed in finding acceptance with God. Let mortal man, clothed in works of law, present himself before the Most High, and His verdict will always be : Unrighteous.'[1]

The first main section of Romans is ended. Paul has exposed ' the sin of man '. He must now declare ' the grace of God '.

9. Nobody can be sure what the Greek verb *proechometha* means here. The choice lies between the AV's ' Are we (the Jews) better than they (the Gentiles)', in which case it repeats v. 1, and the RV's ARE WE IN WORSE CASE THAN THEY? in which case it is an expression of pained surprise from the Jew. But, oddly enough, a decision between them is not important; for if you argue, as Paul does, that Jew

[1] Denney, *Romans, ad loc.*

and Gentile are on the same footing before God, it does
not matter whether you say the Jews are not better off or
not worse off.

20. Through the law cometh the knowledge of sin

'It is the straight-edge of the law that shows us how
crooked we are' (Phillips). One of Paul's aphorisms to be
vividly elucidated in chapter 7. Through the law we become
aware of the sharp contrast between what we ought to do
and what in fact we do. So the law creates a consciousness
of sin; but it cannot show us how to overcome sin.

BUT THE GRACE OF GOD
3.21–8.39

21-26. GOD'S REMEDY FOR SIN

Having diagnosed man's disease, Paul now describes
God's cure. Up till now Paul's theme has been the sin of
man and God's holy displeasure at it. But man's extremity
is God's opportunity. Here the gospel comes in. And the
gospel proclaims, not God's wrath, but his righteousness—
his sovereign power which delivers men from sin, gives them
a new status, empowers them to lead a new life, and kindles
in their hearts an immortal hope.

The passage which follows is among the hardest in Paul's
letters. It will conduce to clearness if we first try to grasp
its main ideas and then elucidate details in notes.

BUT NOW, says Paul, as if with a great sigh of relief, a
new day dawns in which God offers men a righteousness
which could never otherwise have been theirs. What kind
of righteousness is it?

Let us recall that THE RIGHTEOUSNESS OF GOD, for Paul,
means a divine vindicating activity whereby God confers
on men a new status or standing with himself. It is on the
status, rather than the act, that the accent falls in the first
two verses.

Paul describes it first *negatively*. It is *not legal*. Though in complete harmony with the old revelation—THE LAW AND THE PROPHETS—as Paul will show in chapter 4, it does not consist in the attempt to keep all the rules and regulations of the Jewish law.

Next, he describes it *positively*. It comes by FAITH IN JESUS CHRIST; not by achieving but by believing—believing in the living Christ.

Then he describes its form, its basis and its purpose. It takes the *form* of God freely 'justifying' sinners on the score of their faith in Christ's redeeming work. JUSTIFY does not mean '*make* righteous'. It means 'declare righteous', 'acquit', 'set right'. God does what is unheard of in any proper court of law—he acquits guilty men and treats them as righteous. So he gives them a new status— the status of forgiven men, men potentially at least right with God and called to become what they are. (Note: The spiritual truth behind Paul's metaphor is that movingly set forth in the parable of the Prodigal Son. The father taking back his scapegrace son is, in a figure, ' God justifying the ungodly ').

Next, Paul describes the *basis* on which God is able to perform this miracle of grace. It is the REDEMPTION or 'deliverance', wrought in Christ. God, Paul says, SET FORTH the crucified Christ as an 'expiation' (or 'mercy seat': see the notes), i.e. a means of forgiveness for the sinner with faith.

Lastly, Paul describes God's *purpose* in all this. It was to show his righteous character at the present-time—since in the past God had forbearingly 'passed over' men's sins —and reveal himself as JUST, AND THE JUSTIFIER OF HIM THAT HATH FAITH IN JESUS, i.e. as the God who at once deals faithfully with sin and saves sinners who put faith in Jesus.

22. Faith in Jesus Christ

Lit. 'faith of' (AV). But the RV is undoubtedly right. It is an objective genitive.

23. Fall short of the glory of God

The 'glory of God' here is 'man's original estate as created in the likeness of God'. Cf. I Cor. 11.7.

24. His grace

One of Paul's cardinal words. Signifying originally 'charm', it came to mean 'favour' or 'kindness' shown by a superior. In Paul it means the free, unmerited kindness of God to sinners.

Redemption

A metaphor from the slave-market. The Greek *apolytrōsis* originally denoted the 'ransoming' of a slave from bondage by a money payment. Later it came to mean more generally 'deliverance' (e.g. the deliverance from Egypt. Deut. 7.8). The idea here is that God in Christ provides deliverance for his people from the guilt and power of sin.

25. Propitiation (*hilastērion*)

A misleading translation. In biblical Greek the verb *hilaskesthai* means 'expiate', not 'propitiate'. It is a sacrificial term to describe the annulment of sin. We may therefore translate 'expiation' or, better—since God is the agent—'means of forgiveness'. But there is much to be said for the old scholars who took Paul to be referring here to something more specific, viz. 'the mercy seat', or lid of the ark (*kappōreth*), described in Exod. 25. (1) This is the usual meaning of *hilastērion* in the LXX, as it is in the only other NT passage—Heb. 9.5—where the word occurs. (2) IN HIS (*own*) BLOOD favours this view. It was animal blood, not his own which the high-priest sprinkled on the

'mercy seat' on the day of atonement. (3) In Christian
literature outside the NT *hilastērion* always means a 'place'.
If this is right, Paul is saying that Christ crucified has
become for the world what the mercy seat was for Israel.
What was symbolically figured forth on the Day of Atonement has been fulfilled in Christ. Christ on his Cross is the
place where God shows his mercy to all men.

By his blood
goes with PROPITIATION, and is a graphic metaphor for the
Crucifixion.

His righteousness
seems to mean here God's righteous character on which the
sin of the world had, as it were, cast a shadow.

The RV's PASSING OVER is a much better rendering of
the Greek *paresis* than the AV's REMISSION.

26. Just, and the justifier
suggests almost a tension between God's justice and his
mercy. But perhaps the meaning is like Isaiah's 'a
righteous God and a Saviour', i.e. a God who puts things
right and delivers. Paul certainly holds that in the Cross
God is seen dealing faithfully with sin and, at the same
time, saving sinners.

This passage teaches an objective atonement. Whether
we translate 'expiation' or 'mercy seat', Christ crucified is
announced as God's chosen way of mediating forgiveness
to the sinner on the condition of faith, while at the same
time judging sin. But we get no clear rationale of the
Atonement. For further light we must turn to such passages
as II Cor. 5.21.

27-31. TWO INFERENCES AND AN OBJECTION
The first of the two inferences which Paul draws from his
doctrine is that all 'boasting' gets its death-blow. By

'boasting' he means the temper of the Pharisee in the parable (Luke 18.10-14) who 'swanked' of his spiritual achievements before God as though they gave him some claim on the divine favour. There is an end to all that, Paul says, for salvation is not a meritorious achievement but a gift you receive in humble faith from Another. (It is a lesson we still find difficult to learn, so much of the Pharisee lingers in us, so prone are we to rely on our own resources and take pride in our virtue) (27f.).

The second inference is that Jew and Gentile are on the same footing in all this. If justification were by the law, then the Jews who have the law would be specially privileged—and the Gentiles would be God's 'step-bairns'. As it is, however, there is only one God, and only one way of salvation—by faith—for both. (Once again, let us note how difficult we Christians find it to get out of the 'God-of-the-Jews-only' frame of mind. Most of us keep 'a most favoured nation clause' at the back of our minds. Whenever people get talking about the relations between white people and black, it comes out) (29f.).

Finally (31) Paul counters the Jewish objection that his whole system of salvation undermines the law. By the LAW here Paul means the whole revelation of God in the Old Testament (in v. 27 LAW means 'principle'). 'Understand the gospel properly,' he says, 'and you will see that it confirms the deepest principles of the Old Testament, as I propose to show you from the story of Abraham' (31).

IV

'*I will show this from the story of our great forefather. Abraham was accepted by God not for what he did (as though he had earned his acceptance) but for his faith. His acceptance did not depend upon circumcision, for it took place before his circumcision, which followed as a confirming seal. God meant Abraham to number uncircumcised as well as circumcised among his spiritual children.*

The promise to Abraham rested on faith, not law. If doing the law were the condition of securing it, faith and promise would be stultified. (What law produces is not God's blessing but his wrath.) The promise applies to all Abraham's children; so it must depend on faith; for if it depended on law, the Gentiles would be excluded.

Abraham is the father of all true believers. You remember how God named him "a father of many nations" before he even had a son. Though he and Sarah seemed long past having a family, he believed God would honour his promise of a son. This faith God counted to him as righteousness. Now this old story of Abraham's trust in God typifies our Christian faith. We believe in a God who, to save us, gave Jesus to die for our sins and raised him from the dead.'

1-12. ABRAHAM JUSTIFIED BY FAITH

Just when we seem to be leaving the Old Testament behind, Paul harks away back to 'father Abraham' and Genesis. The last verse of chapter 3 shows why. Paul had claimed that the gospel confirmed the old revelation. To confute the Jewish objector, he must make good his claim. So he points to Abraham who, for the Jews, was not only the founder of their race but also the righteous man *par excellence*. How, he asks, did *he* become righteous? Now it was orthodox Jewish teaching that Abraham became righteous because (by anticipation) he kept the law. ABRAHAM KEPT THE LAW OF THE MOST HIGH, AND WAS TAKEN INTO COVENANT WITH HIM (Ecclus. 44.21). What Paul does here is to wrest Abraham from the champions of 'law righteousness' and hold him up as a shining example of the man 'who through faith is righteous'.

He makes two points.

First (1-8) by appeal to Gen. 15.6 (which excellently suits his purpose because it equates faith with righteousness) he shows that Abraham found favour with God for his faith, and not for anything he had done. 'Consult your Bibles,' he says, 'and see what the text says: "Abraham had faith in God, and it was reckoned to him as righteousness."' Note the word RECKONED: it implies that he had no righteousness of his own, but was credited with what he did not have (as the Christian is). Look again at Ps. 32.1f., and you will find David saying the same thing. The blessed man is not the sinless man, but the one whose sins God does not count, the man whose sins he forgives.

Next (9-10) Paul shows that God's acceptance of Abraham did not depend on circumcision. The Jew might object: 'All very well, but Abraham did observe the law, since he received circumcision which is the mark of the man who keeps the law.' 'Open your Bibles again,' Paul replies, 'and you will see that Abraham's circumcision, recorded in Gen. 17.11, came later than his acceptance with God, recorded in Gen. 15.6. True, he was circumcised, but that was only a SEAL affixed afterwards to an acceptance he enjoyed when he was as uncircumcised as any Gentile.'

In all this Paul finds a providential purpose (vv. 11-12). God meant Abraham to be the spiritual father of ALL true believers, both uncircumcised Gentiles and circumcised Jews, who have a faith like Abraham's own.

1. The words HATH FOUND (AV and RV) probably do not belong to the true text. Why OUR FOREFATHER? N~t because Paul's readers were mostly Jews, but because one Jew is arguing with another.

4f. Is not reckoned

A metaphor from book-keeping, reminding us that a man's account may be credited with something he has not fully earned. Paul draws out the implications of this with an illustration from everyday life. He distinguishes between a gift and a wage. When a man does a bit of work, he can claim his wage as a rightful due. GRACE does not come into the picture. A gift, because it has not been earned, is quite different. And so in the present case: when righteousness is reckoned, or credited, to a man, it is not because he has earned it. So God deals with us. God WHO JUSTIFIETH THE UNGODLY. Paul's gospel in a nutshell. 'What could I do,' said Thomas Chalmers, 'if God did not justify the ungodly?'

13-25. ABRAHAM GOT THE PROMISE THROUGH FAITH

Paul's argument in these verses is that the famous Promise of blessing came to Abraham through faith, not law; that the People of the Promise, not the People of the Law, may rightly regard him as their spiritual father; and that Abraham's faith in God, who gives life to the dead, typifies Christian faith.

First, in vv. 13-15, Paul raises the question, Does inheriting the Promise depend on law or faith? His answer is: 'On faith.' This he proves by showing the absurdity of the alternative: 'On law.' A promise dependent on keeping a law which no man can keep is a chimaera. What the law does is to condemn a man, not bless him.

The fact that the Promise depends on faith shows (v. 16) that God meant it for *all* Abraham's descendants—Gentiles

with a faith like Abraham's as well as Jewish possessors of
the law. Abraham is therefore the spiritual ancestor of all
who inherit the Promise by faith.

Then (17-22) Paul characterizes Abraham's faith as faith
in God who brings life from the dead. When Abraham and
Sarah seemed too old to have a family, God promised them
a wonderful progeny. It seemed impossible. But, against
all the odds, Abraham took God at his word, and his faith,
instead of wilting, grew ever stronger. This triumphant
faith God counted to him for righteousness. Abraham had
honoured God by believing; God honoured Abraham for
his faith.

Finally (vv. 23-25) Paul applies his argument. The story
of the patriarch's acceptance by God typifies our Christian
experience. We are justified in the same way. Like
Abraham, we put our faith in a God who brings life from
the dead—brings to life again a Saviour who was crucified
for our sins.

This chapter, with its very rabbinical dialectic may seem,
at first sight, without relevance for us. And yet it is
valuable for the light it throws on Paul's conception of
faith. To begin with, he shows that faith is something
which did not begin with Christianity, but lies deep at the
heart of all true religion. In the second place, he illumines
the nature of faith. Essentially, it is a taking of God at his
word—an Abraham-like obedience, in face of all odds, to the
God who reveals himself to us. Now, since God has revealed
himself to us decisively in Christ, Christian faith is a taking
of God at his word in Christ: the decision to live no more by
reliance on our own resources, but only by trust in his saving
grace offered to us in Christ. ' The one right thing to do in
presence of the revelation and appeal of God in Christ is to
stake one's life upon it for good and all. This was what
Abraham did when he believed God, and this is always what
faith means in the Bible. Without it, it is impossible to
please God; but where He finds it, He asks for nothing more.

He counts his faith to the believer for righteousness; and in very truth the man who so believes is right with God.'[1]

George Macdonald somewhere describes an old man in an ill-lit cottage calling a child in from the road; and she goes, groping and following the sound, till she feels his hand on her head. ' Noo, my lass,' he says, ' ye'll ken what faith means. When God tells you to gang in the mirk, gang.' Such was Abraham's faith; such is the Christian's; but for the latter the ' mirk ' is irradiated by the fact of Christ.

13. The promise, etc.

The promise that Abraham should have a son and descendants like the stars of heaven (Gen. 12.2, 15.5, 17.16).

14. If they which are of the law be heirs, faith is made void

(because it is not called for) **and the promise is made of none effect** (because no man is able to keep the law).

15.

An aside. The law only produces the sin and retribution of chapters 1 and 2.

Where there is no law, etc.

There may be sin where there is no law; but where there is a law, sin becomes transgression, something with guilt attaching to it.

17.

Gen. 17.5 (LXX).

18. Who against hope, etc.

' While the world around him cried " No ", Abraham cried " Yes ", because he was supported by the Word of God.'[2]

So shall thy seed be

Gen. 15.5. so: like the stars.

[1] Denney, *The Way Everlasting*, 260.
[2] Barth, *Romans*, 142.

19. Tr. with RSV: 'He did not weaken in faith when he considered his own body, which was as good as dead because he was about a hundred years old, or when he considered the barrenness of Sarah's womb.'

25. Who was delivered up

The words echo what was said of the Suffering Servant (Isa. 53.12. LXX). The contrast between DELIVERED UP and RAISED is formal, not logical. Paul means: 'He died and rose that we might be saved from our sins.'

V

'*Justification brings peace with God—and a heavenly hope.
As a result, our very hardships take on new meaning. Nor
is this an illusion, for, through the Holy Spirit, we experience
God's love flooding our hearts.*

*What a love it is, signally shown in Christ's death for us
unworthy men! If, when we were God's enemies, Christ
died for us, surely he will save us now that we are friends.
This is something to make us exult.*

*One man involved the race in sin and death. Redemption,
coming also through one Man, makes a contrast to the Fall.
The Fall, starting from one sin, brought condemnation:
Redemption, starting from many, brought forgiveness. If
the deadly effects of Adam's work are plain, still plainer are
the life-giving ones of Christ's. One man sinned—a whole
race suffered for it: one Man lived righteously—a whole
race gains life by it. Again, one man disobeyed—all became
sinners: one Man obeyed—all may become righteous. What
place has the law in this? It was an afterthought, designed
to multiply transgressions. But if sin thus increased, much
more so did God's grace; for he determined to oust the
tyrants, sin and death, and to set grace and life upon the
throne.*'

In the previous chapters, Paul described man's need of
justification and how God has met his need in Christ. But
justification is not the whole story; it is rather the first step
on the road to salvation. So in chapters 5-8 Paul describes
the happy fruits of justification: victory over sin's power,
the new life lived with the Spirit's help, the blessed hope of
immortality.

The meaning is the same if we say, in the words of

Habakkuk, that chapters 1-4 deal with 'he who through faith is righteous' and 5-8 with 'shall live'.

1-11. THE HAPPY FRUITS OF JUSTIFICATION

First (1-4) Paul describes our new life as justified sinners. Justification brings PEACE WITH GOD, i.e. reconciliation, with its resultant sense of inner serenity. Since Christ ushers us into the Father's presence—that is the meaning of ACCESS— we are on a new footing with God, a footing not of hostility but of favour—THIS GRACE IN WHICH WE STAND. And this state of grace carries with it the exultant hope of THE GLORY OF GOD—that we shall attain hereafter the perfection and beatitude God designed for us. Does this mean that the present is dark? On the contrary, our very hardships wear a 'new look'. Instead of being meaningless, hardships breed PATIENCE (better, 'endurance'—the virtue of the martyrs); and through this discipline, this being hammered on the anvil of trial without going to pieces, we acquire *dokimē*, lit. 'testedness', i.e. ripeness of character, the temper of the hardened veteran. This, in turn, crowning the golden chain, leads to HOPE.

This hope, Paul continues (4-7), can be relied on, because it rests on THE LOVE OF GOD—a love which is a present reality, which is in fact what we know as the experience of the Holy Spirit. How great a thing that love is, Christ's death for us helpless sinners declares. To show its wonder, Paul employs an illustration. He contrasts the rigidly RIGHTEOUS man (somebody like Cato the Censor) and the really GOOD man (shall we say Francis of Assisi?). For the former it is hardly conceivable that anybody would care to sacrifice his life; you might find someone, in a noble moment, daring to die for a person of quite exceptional worthiness like the latter. But no such worthiness in us evoked the sacrifice of Christ. Christ died not for just men or even good men, but for bad men. This is the measure of God's love for us. (Just so, in the Gospels, Jesus says that God is 'kind even to the ungrateful and evil' and himself is known as 'the friend of publicans and sinners'.)

Finally (9-11), Paul draws the conclusion of all this for the Christian's final destiny. The love that went the length of the Cross for our redeeming may be trusted to see us safely through the Last Judgment. If, when we were enemies, the crucified Christ made us God's friends, how much more will the living Christ save us at the last.

1. Did Paul write WE HAVE (*echomen*) PEACE (AV) *or* LET US HAVE (*echōmen*) PEACE (RV)? In Greek it is the difference between a short 'o' and a long 'o', two vowels that, especially in dictation, were easily confused. The MSS. evidence strongly favours the RV. But this is a case where, in our judgment, 'the internal evidence of readings' is to be preferred to 'the external evidence of manuscripts'. Inference, not exhortation, is Paul's purpose here. Therefore our vote goes (with that of the RSV) for WE HAVE. By the same reasoning we prefer the AV's WE . . . REJOICE and WE GLORY in vv. 2 and 3 to the RV's LET US REJOICE and LET US ALSO REJOICE.

2. This grace:
This 'position of favour' (Weymouth).

5. The love of God
A subjective genitive, as the grammarians say. God's love for us, not our love for God.

Given:
At baptism.

6. Weak:
Helpless to save ourselves: 'the state of despairing impotence Bunyan so vividly describes in the opening sentences of *The Pilgrim's Progress*.'

In due season:

At the fitting time, the time fixed by God. Cf. Gal. 4.4.

8. Commendeth

Better, 'shows' or 'proves'. 'The classic text on the
oneness of God's love and Christ's Cross. Christ's action
is God's action. Christ's love is God's love.'[1] Said the
boy Bevis (in Richard Jefferies' tale) as he looked at a
picture of the Crucifixion, 'If God had been there, he
wouldn't have let them do it!' If Paul is sure of anything,
it is that God *was* there.

10. Shall we be saved by his life:

By the living Christ, by 'Christ in us the hope of glory'.
It is Paul's equivalent of BECAUSE I LIVE, YE SHALL LIVE
ALSO (John 14.19).

11. The RV's RECONCILIATION (which is better than the
AV's ATONEMENT) is a comprehensive term for the restora-
tion of the sinner from estrangement to fellowship with
God.

12-21. ADAM AND CHRIST

Having spoken of Christ the Saviour, Paul pauses here to
consider the relation of Redemption to the Fall, comparing
Christ with Adam. This comparison enables him to show
the universal range of Christ's saving work. From Adam,
he says, came sin and death for his descendants; from Christ
comes righteousness and life for all who believe in him.
And always grace is mightier than sin.

But if the general drift of the passage is plain, the details
are difficult, especially in the opening verses (12-14). THERE-
FORE, AS THROUGH ONE MAN SIN ENTERED INTO THE WORLD,
AND DEATH THROUGH SIN, AND SO DEATH PASSED UNTO ALL

---

[1] Nygren, *Romans*, 201f.

MEN, FOR THAT ALL SINNED. . . . Paul begins to draw
his parallel between Adam and Christ, but he does not
complete it. What he intended to say was: 'so also by
one man righteousness entered the world, and life by
righteousness.'

But let us study what he does say. AS THROUGH ONE
MAN SIN ENTERED INTO THE WORLD. Paul acknowledges the
fateful—and fatal—role played by our first father: the
presence of sin in the world is due to Adam's primal disobedience to God's command. Paul of course took the
Genesis story as literal history: before him lay the sacred
record of how God said to Adam concerning the tree of
the knowledge of good and evil, THOU SHALT NOT EAT OF IT,
FOR IN THE DAY THAT THOU EATEST THEREOF THOU SHALT
SURELY DIE. Adam disobeyed and sin found a foothold in
the world. Next, AND THROUGH SIN DEATH. That DEATH
was sin's inevitable concomitant and penalty, Paul believed
along with his Jewish contemporaries. Adam's act let that
too loose in the world. But let us pay particular attention
to the words that follow: AND SO DEATH PASSED UNTO ALL
MEN FOR THAT ALL SINNED (eph'hō pantes hēmarton). The
last four words mean 'because all sinned' (cf. 3.23), and the
plain meaning is that death extended its sway to all men
because all men were, in point of fact, sinners. Paul does
not say (as many of the doctors of the Church from Augustine supposed him to say) 'in whom all sinned', as though
all men sinned implicitly in Adam's sin and were punished
for his disobedience. He does not speak of Adam's
descendants inheriting a debt of sinfulness from Adam. His
view is rather that sin is the responsible act of every man,
but that when he sins, as he does, he comes under the power
of sin and death which Adam's act let loose in the world
and from which, save through Christ, no man may escape.

We cannot of course, unless we are fundamentalists, sub-
scribe *in toto* to this part of Paul's doctrine. The truth is
that we do not know the origin of sin; we only know that

it is here. But if we interpret the Genesis story of the Fall
differently from Paul, it remains for us 'a true myth' in the
sense that the story of Adam and Eve is the story of you
and me—we are sinful and fallen beings who stand in need
of the 'redemption which is in Christ Jesus'.

We may now go on to vv. 13-14. Paul suddenly en-
counters a difficulty. Is not the time before Moses an
exception to the statement that all have sinned? No, he
answers, there was sin in the world before Moses. True, if
the law does not exist, sin is not *imputed*—marked up to
one's account. Nevertheless death, which is the penalty
of sin, held sway over the men who lived between Adam
and Moses, even if they did not sin as Adam did (viz. by
breaking an express prohibition with a death penalty
attached to it). Now, where you have the penalty, you
must also have the offence. Therefore the time before
Moses is no exception.

WHO IS A FIGURE OF HIM THAT WAS TO COME. FIGURE
is lit. 'type'; in theological language, a person (or event) in
history corresponding to another. Paul means that in the
immense influence which his action had the first Adam fore-
shadowed the second.

The next three verses (15-17) unfold the differences
between the Fall and Redemption. THE FREE GIFT (of
righteousness), Paul says, 'was not like the trespass.' One
brought ruin to many, the other blessing. The Fall, starting
from one transgression, resulted in condemnation: Redemption, issuing from many transgressions, has resulted in forgiveness. The Fall produced death: Redemption produces
life. Only notice the MUCH MORE of vv. 15 and 17: the
implication is that grace is far mightier than sin.

This passage has much to say about the solidarity of men
in evil—a fact which has been ruthlessly forced home on
us to-day by the grim logic of history. But if we are bound
together for ill, Paul says here that we are also bound
together for good. For 'what Christ has done can alter the

character of every single person and can transform the nature of the common life which all men share together.'

At last, in 18f., Paul completes his parallel between Adam and Christ. One man did wrong—all men were condemned for it. One man did right—all men may be saved by what he did. One man's disobedience made all men sinners— one man's obedience will make many righteous.

The comparison between Adam and Christ is over. But in the middle, between the two, stood the law. What place had it in the Divine Plan? 'The law slipped in' (*pareiselthen*) Paul answers (v. 20)—it was a parenthesis, or afterthought, in the divine plan. Its purpose was to increase sin by making it flagrant transgression. Is it absurd to say that God's curb on sin became almost a goad? No, God designed that sin should come to its full height before he dealt with it. 'Where sin abounded, grace super-abounded.' Where sin and death ruled supreme, God willed that, through Christ, grace and life should occupy the throne.

15. Many:
means practically all, but stresses that the all are not few.

16. Justification
The Greek *dikaiōma* means here ' acquittal '.

18. Act of righteousness
The same Greek word *dikaiōma*, but with a different meaning. Christ's work is seen as something in which righteousness was embodied.

Justification of life:
Pardon and salvation.

19. The obedience of the one:
Christ's life of perfect obedience consummated on the Cross (Phil. 2.8).

VI

'*If more sin brings more grace, shall we go on sinning?
Never! Sin flatly contradicts all that Christian baptism
signifies. This rite not only brings us into union with Christ,
but also enables us to share in his death and resurrection.
As Christ by dying on the Cross lost all contact with sin, so
we, united with Christ in baptism, have finished with sin and
risen into new life. Act then as men who have renounced
sin's lordship, and consecrate all your faculties to God and
righteousness.*

*Does freedom from law mean freedom to sin? Never!
It means freedom to do right. Take an illustration from
slavery. Think of conversion as a change of masters
(nobody, remember, can be a slave to two). Once you were
sin's slaves, and your business wickedness. Now you have
become slaves of righteousness and your task is to grow in
holiness. Freed from sin, you are the slaves of God. The
wage your old master paid was death; your new master
makes you a present of eternal life.*'

Rom. 5-8, as we saw, describes the new life of the Christian
following his justification. If this was not very clear in
chapter 5, it becomes so now. Chapters 6 and 7 discuss the
negative meaning of the new life, viz. its freedom from sin
and the law (6 being mostly concerned with sin and 7 with
the law), whereas Paul's theme in chapter 8 is its *positive*
meaning, as a life controlled and empowered by the Holy
Spirit.[1]

1-14. DYING AND RISING WITH CHRIST

Paul had just let fall a true but perilous word: ' Where sin

[1] John Knox, *The Interpreter's Bible*, 9, 470.

abounded grace did much more abound.' It is not hard
to imagine some wrong-headed person drawing the conclusion: 'Very well then, if to multiply sin is to multiply
God's grace, let us go on sinning. It will give God his great
chance.'

Earlier, in 3.8, Paul had touched on this mischievous per-
version of his teaching. It is the heresy that the man who
is 'saved' can do, morally, pretty well what he likes.
Antinomianism is its name; and whenever Paul's gospel of
justification by faith, not by works, has been powerfully
preached, it has tended to raise its ugly head. So it was,
for example, in the early days of Methodism—thus we read
in Southey's life of Wesley: [1]

'There were members of the Society who spoke in the
most glorious manner of Christ, and of their interest in his
complete salvation, and yet were indulging the most un-
christian tempers, and living in the greatest immoralities.'

But Methodism has had no monopoly of it; it is a danger
against which Evangelical Christianity in every age and
place has had to guard.

Paul comes down on it like a hammer. 'Continue in sin!
Never! How can we who died to sin go on living in it? Or
have you completely misunderstood the meaning of your
conversion and baptism?' So he proceeds to describe the
believer's dying with Christ to his old life of sin and rising
with him into a completely new one, as if to say: 'Anyone
who has really understood what his baptism means—a clean
and final break with the old bad life—would never draw
this fantastic conclusion.'

This is Paul's chief point in this passage, but his words
about Baptism are so difficult that we must elucidate them
carefully. His argument, simplified, is this:

(1) Our baptism was a real sharing in Christ's death and
resurrection, so that we are now living in a new order of
life (3-5, 8-9).

[1] p. 328.

(2) Since Christ's death was a dying out from under sin's power (see the notes), we who died with him have (in principle) won clear of sin's dominion (10, 6-7).

(3) Therefore, as members of Christ's Body, we are called to live out what we really are—men dead to sin and alive for God and righteousness (11-14).

Paul is using the familiar symbolism of baptism (by immersion, of course, and of adult believers) for a practical purpose; but his 'mystical' description of it as a dying and rising with Christ, has led some scholars to detect here the influence on his thought of the Greek mystery religions, with their notions of a dying and rising cult-god in whose destiny the initiate ritually shares. This is improbable.

We must remember, to begin with, the paramountcy of faith in Paul's gospel. He does not regard baptism as another way, co-ordinate with faith, of appropriating salvation. Rather, he sees the familiar stages of baptism—descent into the pool, submersion and emersion—as unfolding the deepest meanings of faith, which is a 'planting' of the man in Christ so that he shares in the virtue of what his Saviour has done for him.

Next, we must remember that baptism embodies the historic gospel of Christ crucified and risen. Or, to put it in other words, 'behind Christian baptism stands the baptism of Christ himself (Mark 10.38, Luke 12.50), unique and all-inclusive, undertaken by Christ himself for the sins of the whole world'.[1] It is into the virtue of this once-for-all baptism that a man enters when he is 'baptized into Christ'.

Finally, if we remember the Jewish conceptions of 'corporate personality' and 'prophetic symbolism' we can forget about the Greek Mysteries.

For Paul, baptism 'into Christ' means that the believer enters into a faith-relationship with Christ. But it means more. Christ is the Head, or inclusive representative, of the new People of God—the Church—which forms with him a

[1] W. F. Flemington, *The New Testament Doctrine of Baptism*, 73.

corporate personality. Baptism therefore means being incorporated into Christ's Body and so sharing in the saving acts of him who is ' the Saviour of the Body '.

The ' realism ' of his language (for clearly ' dying ' and ' rising ' here are more than mere picture-phrases) strongly recalls the symbolic actions practised by the Old Testament prophets, e.g. Jeremiah. As the prophet's act is no mere acted parable but a real, though partial, entering into the divine purpose and helping it forward, so Christian baptism is a real, though partial, accomplishment (through the Spirit) of God's saving action in Christ: in short, ' an effective sign ', a sacrament.

Not that Paul believes the rite acts magically, without the need of faith, or that it instantly transforms sinners into saints. In baptism a man is freed from sin (conceived as a semi-personal power), not made morally perfect. By it he passes out of sin's dominion into Christ's. Yet even in this new *milieu*, he has to ' fight the good fight ', since he remains ' in the flesh '. This is why, at the end of this section, Paul exhorts him to ' reckon himself DEAD UNTO SIN BUT ALIVE UNTO GOD, and to consecrate all his MEMBERS—his faculties, we might say—to righteousness.

5. ' But if we have been united with him in a death like this, we shall certainly be united with him in a resurrection like his ' (RSV).

6. Our old man:
Our unregenerate self.

The body of sin:
The body belonging to sin, which is sin's tool.

7. Just as no legal claim can be made on a dead man, so one who is (ethically) dead IS JUSTIFIED—has his quittance— from any claim that sin could make on him.

E

8f. Union with Christ carries with it the assurance of immortality. Paul does not, like Plato, teach the natural immortality of the soul. Our faith-union with the living Christ is our pledge of the life immortal.

10. He died unto sin once

While Christ lived, he had relations with sin (though he was sinless). When he died, these stopped. (Sin could never make him his victim again.) So, while we lived, we also had relations with sin (different from his). Now that we have died, these relations of ours must also cease.

11. In Christ Jesus

The first example in Romans of Paul's famous phrase. What does being 'in Christ' mean? To reply that it describes the believer's intimate personal communion with his living Lord is true, but not enough. For Christ here signifies a corporate personality, and to be 'in Christ' is to be in his Body—to be a member of the new People of God of which he is the living and regnant Head.

12-14. A practical re-inforcement of vv. 1-11. 'You are new men in Christ,' Paul says in effect, 'therefore renounce the sins (especially the carnal ones) of your old pagan life. The power of sin in you is broken. Become what you are—men who have died to sin and risen into new life.'

For ye are not under law, but under grace:

You are not living under a gloomy code of restraints but in the sunshine of God's favour.

15-23. AN ILLUSTRATION FROM SLAVERY

Still attacking Antinomianism, Paul takes an analogy from slavery. It is not one of his best, for it limps in places.

The very suggestion that freedom from law means freedom to sin is absurd, he says. Let them regard their

conversion *as a change of masters*. It is a law governing all
service that the slave must yield his master exclusive obedience: no man may be a slave to two at the same time. In
the matter at issue they have to choose between serving Sin
(personified as a slave-holder) and serving Righteousness.
(In 16b for 'righteousness' he awkwardly writes OBEDIENCE.)
One service leads to death; the other to life. As Christians,
they have made their choice. They have left master Sin
for master Righteousness. Now, although a man may
change his service, he cannot give up his obligation to serve.
If they have been freed from Sin's service, they are bound
to be slaves to Righteousness. (Here, v. 19, Paul apologizes
for his analogy. 'Slavery to righteousness' is hardly a
happy description of the Christian life. But, human nature
being the weak thing it is, analogies like this are necessary.)

Then he applies his analogy. If Christians are as
exclusively bound in their new service as they were in their
old, they must make their actions correspond. Instead of
devoting their faculties to evil-doing, they must now devote
them to well-doing, aiming ever to grow in holiness. To
decide which is the true service, they need only compare
the results they yield. What they got from their old service
were only things they now blush to remember. What they
get from their new service is growth in holiness, with eternal
life as their goal.

He sums all up in a splendid antithesis. The wage
(*opsōnia*: the word used of a soldier's pay) Sin pays his man
is death; but the free-gift (*charisma*) God gives his servant
is eternal life in Christ Jesus our Lord.

16. Servants

Though our English versions render the Greek word
doulos by 'servant', we should really translate it by 'slave'.
For ancient slavery was a much more exclusive relationship
than our modern service. Nowadays a man *can* serve two
masters—he may sit at one employer's desk by day, and

fiddle in another's orchestra by night.   No slave could do this.

17. That form of teaching

refers to the instruction in Christian moral principles which the apostles gave their converts.

19. Iniquity unto iniquity:

Ever increasing iniquity.

22. Eternal life:

The life of the new ' aeon ', or age, begun with the coming of Christ but to be consummated in glory.   The phrase denotes life of a new quality, life with the tang of eternity about it, life that can never die.   It is St. John's favourite expression for the chief blessing of the gospel.

VII

' Likewise, we are freed from the law. Death ends law's power, as you can see from the example of a woman whose husband has died—by the death the living gains freedom. So with us. A death—Christ's—has taken place, and as a result, we who have died with him are free to live the new good life God expects of us. This, impossible in the old life because of the sinful passions aroused by the law, now becomes possible because we live under the control of God's Spirit, and not under the old written code.

It is wrong to call the law sin; yet it does make man conscious of sin, even provoke him to it. Take the Tenth Commandment. So deeply is human nature in sin's grip that ' Thou shalt not covet' is enough to make a man say ' I will'. For a time a man may live in blissful ignorance of law. Then comes the commandment, sin springs to life, and the man is ruined. Thus sin turns God's intended blessing, the law, into a curse.

The law is spiritual, but I am frail flesh, prone to sin. I can see the good and desire it, but do it I cannot. My better self recognizes the law of God, but I break it through this sin which inhabits my flesh. There seems to be one law for my conscience, the law of God, and another for my outward conduct, the law of sin and death. Is there any hope of deliverance for my misery? Praise be to God there is—in Christ.'

1-6. ILLUSTRATION FROM MARRIAGE

The theme of 6 was the Christian's freedom from the power of sin. The theme of 7 is that he is free also from the power of the law.

Everybody conversant with law, Paul says, knows that the power of law over a person ceases with death. Take a simple illustration from marriage. On her husband's death the wife, who during his lifetime was bound to him, is freed. The same is true of ourselves. We Christians are the living who have been freed by death from the law. The death was Christ's, and we who have died with him (in baptism) are freed from the law. Now united to the living Christ we are meant to BRING FORTH FRUIT—live holy lives—for God. In our old carnal life the sinful passions excited by the law made us BRING FORTH FRUIT for death. Now that we are delivered from it, we can serve God in a new way, the way of the Spirit and not of the old code of statutes.

(Many scholars treat this simple illustration in 2-3 as an allegory of which each term has to bear a significant meaning in the application of 4-6. In this allegory they find, for example, that it is the husband (the law) who dies, whereas in the application it is the woman (ourselves). So they convict Paul of bungling. This allegorizing is quite unnecessary.)

1. Over a man (*anthrōpou*):
Better: ' Over a person.'

4. Ye also were made dead to the law through the body of Christ
What does THE BODY OF CHRIST mean here? His crucified body? A reference to the Cross is not excluded. But BODY should probably be spelt here with a capital B, as referring to the mystical Body. By incorporation at baptism into the mystical Body of Christ, we shared in the death of Christ, the Body's Head. Because Christ died to the law, so do we. The thought is like that of 6.1-11.

5. The sinful passions which were through the law
Better: ' the sinful passions excited by the law '. Paul will tell us more about them before the chapter is finished.

6. Having died to that wherein we were holden (*kateicho-metha*).

What mantrap is this which 'held us down'? Probably, the law, though some say 'the old sinful state'.

7-13. THE LAW AND SIN

A man who talks of 'the sinful passions excited by the law' lays himself wide open to the charge of identifying the law and sin. Paul passionately denies the very suggestion but admits a fatal link between them: I HAD NOT KNOWN SIN EXCEPT THROUGH THE LAW. Then he plunges into a psychological study of sin and the law in which the first personal pronoun 'I' bulks large.

The question arises: In these verses are we reading autobiography, or is Paul speaking quite generally, despite his 'I'? Since Paul hardly ever says 'I' unless he means himself, and since his phrases seem to reflect the remembered anguish of his own soul, we cannot exclude the autobiographical element. On the other hand, the echoes (especially in v. 11) of the story of Adam's Fall (the word COMMANDMENT, Sin as a personal power recalling the serpent, the verb BEGUILED, the connexion between the sinful deed and death) demand a wider reference. Paul is thinking of *everyman* as well as of himself. It is his own spiritual history, but *universalized*.

It was the law which first showed Paul the true nature of sin (v. 7). The law not only brings knowledge of sin, it stimulates transgression. The Tenth Commandment not only tells a man that coveting is wrong but somehow stirs in him the desire to have what is forbidden. 'Gainsay,' says one of Mary Webb's characters, 'and the blood's on fire.' But our classical illustration here is Augustine and the pears. (He tells how, one stormy night, he and his chums raided a neighbour's orchard. 'They were nice pears,' he comments, 'but it was not the wretched pears my soul coveted, for I had plenty better at home. I picked them simply because

I wanted to be a thief. What was it I loved in the theft? Was it the pleasure of acting against the law in order that I, a prisoner under rules, might have a maimed counterfeit of freedom by doing with impunity what was forbidden, with a dim similitude of omnipotence? '[1]) This is what Paul means when he says (v. 8): SIN FINDING OCCASION (*aphormē:* a base of operations) THROUGH THE COMMANDMENT WROUGHT IN ME ALL MANNER OF COVETING (*epithumia:* illicit desire generally): FOR APART FROM THE LAW SIN IS DEAD.

I WAS ALIVE APART FROM THE LAW ONCE, Paul proceeds (v. 9), thinking no doubt of his boyhood but also surely of Adam's primal innocence. 'Paul sees in his own early childhood a reliving of the Eden story.' What he gives us is *ideal* biography, like Vaughan's:

> *Happy those early days when I*
> *Shined in my angel infancy.*

So, across the later years of moral conflict, we tend to see our childhood. But the 'little angels' we fondly recall were often anything but incarnations of innocence, as any 'nanny' will testify. And there is no period in life to which a man can look back as the time when he had no conscience. Still, there comes a day when we come rudely up against the demands of the moral law, and then, as Paul says, the trouble begins. . . . SIN (so long dormant and apparently dead) REVIVED, AND I DIED, is how he puts it. I DIED means 'I died the living death of sin, precursor of eternal death.'[2]

What a tragic paradox is here (v. 10)—God's command-ment designed to lead men to life (Lev. 18.5, 'My statutes . . . by doing which a man shall *live*') has become a weapon of death in the hand of sin! (Althaus comments:[3]

---

[1] Dodd's translation.

[2] Sanday and Headlam, *Romans, ad loc.*

[3] *Der Brief an die Römer, ad loc.*

'How differently Paul judges man's meeting with the commandment from all ethical idealists like Kant!')

Now, at v. 12, Paul answers the question he had posed in
v. 7. IS THE LAW SIN? 'On the contrary,' he replies, 'it is
holy and good.' Here we may imagine someone demurring,

'Yet, on your own showing, it has led to man's ruin. How
can you honestly call it good?' 'No,' Paul rejoins, 'it was
not the good law but *sin* using the good law which wrought
the damage.' That is certainly a misuse of the law, but in
all this God's purpose is not thwarted. This misuse has
set forth sin in its true colours, as something which turns
God's intended blessing—the law—into a curse. It stands
revealed as EXCEEDING SINFUL, a power ripe for vanquish-
ment by grace.

14-25. THE POWER OF SIN IN THE FLESH

In the last passage we saw that the 'I' must be, to some
extent, autobiographical, though Paul presents his own case
as typical of everyman's. The same is true of the pronoun
in this section. But here another question arises: Do these
verses describe the Christian life, or the life of a man before
his conversion? Is the man in question under law or under
grace? Both views have had their advocates.

1. Commentators from Luther to Nygren hold that Paul
is describing the Christian life. They bid us note that the
tenses are present, not past; that the verses belong to a
section (chapters 5-8) which deals with the Christian life;
and that, on Paul's view, the Christian life is not devoid of
tensions (cf. Rom. 8.23, 'We ourselves groan inwardly').

2. An even longer line of scholars (numbering Denney,
Dodd and Bultmann among the moderns) hold that Paul is
describing a man's condition before his conversion, especially a man under the law. They argue that phrases like
SOLD UNDER SIN and O WRETCHED MAN THAT I AM are, to
say the least, not the normal ejaculations of a converted
man, and that the contrast between chapters 7 and 8 is that

between defeat and victory. And they ask, What would
be the use of conversion if it did not end the spiritual misery
of 14-25?

The second view undoubtedly comes nearer the truth, but
it is not wholly satisfactory. It hardly explains the present
tenses; it has to suppose that 25b is out of place (though not
a MS. says so); and its advocates are apt to assume that the
Christian life is free from spiritual conflict.

Therefore it is best to say (with L. H. Mitton[1]) that 14-25
describe not only a man's pre-conversion state but the
similar experience which may befall a Christian when, for-
getting to live in daily dependence on divine grace, he re-
lapses into reliance on his own resources. Note the *autos
ego* of 25b. This means, ' I, relying on my own resources ',
' I, left to myself ' (Moffatt). 14-25 therefore depict not only
the man under the law but the Christian who slips back into
a legalistic attitude to God. The present tenses describe not
merely a past experience but one which is potentially ever
present. On this view, 25b sums up 14-25, as 25a paves the
way for chapter 8.

We may now turn to the exegesis.

First (14-20), Paul analyses the spiritual struggle of the
man without Christ.

Is the law to blame for procuring man's ruin? No, we
all KNOW THAT THE LAW IS SPIRITUAL (i.e., like God who ' is
spirit '). The reason is that man (Paul says ' I ', presenting
his own case as typical) is made of frail flesh and therefore
in sin's power. His own actions mystify him—he cannot
find his real self in them, for they are the very opposite of
what he wills. Yet his protest against his actions proves
that a part of him is on the law's side. What then? It is
not his true self which performs the actions but that strange
power, sin, ' squatting ' in his flesh. No good thing dwells
in him—or, more accurately, in his *flesh*—his weak human
nature where sin lodges. Willing is one thing; doing, quite

[1] *Expository Times*, Feb. 1954.

another; and though he has the best of intentions, he finds
himself doing evil.

Thus Paul describes the inner life of man as yet un-
touched by the life of Christ. We are reminded of Ovid's
Video meliora proboque Deteriora sequor—only this is far
more poignant. It is a study in divided personality, a personality in dire need of what the psychologists call 'inte-
gration'. Man's inner life appears as a Jekyll-and-Hyde
affair. Dr. Jekyll, the man's true, better self assents to its
highest God-given intuitions and ideals, and yet is power-
less to fulfil them because of that other strange occupant
of his 'soul's dark cottage', whom Stevenson calls Mr.
Hyde. His Pauline name is Sin, and he uses weak human
nature (the flesh) to defeat his higher self. IT IS NO MORE
I—the real I—THAT DO IT, Paul comments, BUT SIN THAT
DWELLETH IN ME.

Then, in vv. 21-23, Paul sums up the situation. Note that
he uses the word 'law' in two senses. In v. 22 the law is
God's law; in v. 21 and v. 23 law means 'principle'. Two principles, then, struggle for mastery in man's nature—a higher
and a lower—producing deadly strife. On the higher side
of his nature, man delights in the law of God ('That,' comments Althaus,[1] 'is the greatest thing Paul can say of un-
redeemed man.'); but he finds another 'principle' at work
in his members, waging war on his MIND (better: 'reason',
the reasoning part of his conscience) and making him sin's
prisoner.

All this is summarized in 25b. SO THEN I BY MYSELF
(without Christ's help) WITH MY MIND SERVE THE LAW OF
GOD, BUT WITH THE FLESH, THE LAW OF SIN. If earlier
(see vv. 17 and 20) Paul almost seemed to shuffle out of his
responsibility by laying the blame on sin, he accepts it fully
here.

Of what avail then is man's delight in God's law if,
because of sin in the flesh, he is impotent to fulfil it? Utterly

[1] *Ibid., ad loc.*

wretched—and wretched just because he knows what God
wants him to be—he is moved to cry, 'Who will rescue me
from the body on which sin has laid its death-grip?' It
is 'a wail of anguish and a cry for help'. The cry is
answered by a ringing *Laus Deo* which proclaims that the
longed-for Deliverer has come: 'God be thanked (I am
delivered), through Jesus Christ our Lord!' 'When he
could do nothing, God did everything, and all that was
left was to give God thanks.'[1] The next chapter will tell
us what God has done, is doing, and will do.

17. No more I . . . but sin

'It is safe for a Christian like Paul—it is not safe for
everybody—to explain his failings by the watchword, Not I
but indwelling sin. That might be antinomian, or mani-
chean, as well as evangelical. A true saint may say it in a
moment of passion, but a sinner had better not make it a
principle.'[2]

22. The inward man

The side of man's nature akin to God.

25. I thank God

The better reading is: 'Thanks be to God.'

[1] Dodd, *Romans, ad loc.*
[2] Denney, *Romans, ad loc.*

VIII

PARAPHRASE

'For those who are Christ's people then, the doom is lifted. The Spirit of life in Christ frees them from sin and death. What the law, weakened by the flesh, could not do, God did in Christ incarnate and crucified, and now we live in the power not of the flesh but of the Spirit. Men can live in two ways—by the flesh or by the Spirit. One way leads to death, the other to life. Now you have God's Spirit in you, and it is your pledge of life immortal. This hope lays us under obligation to live the way life lies—in the Spirit. Led by the Spirit, we are no longer slaves but sons, and thus admitted to God's family, we are heirs with Christ of God's glory.

With that glory present suffering is not to be compared. As nature shared in the blight of man's Fall, so it will share in his Redemption. Presently it sighs in pain, as we do our-selves; but we have the pledge of the Spirit, and hopefully await the complete redemption of man and all things. Meanwhile, the Spirit aids our prayers, and God's chosen may count on his co-operation in all circumstances.

God is on our side. The Christ who died and rose on our behalf now intercedes for us in heaven. If God gave his only Son to save us, we may trust him to give us everything else, and nothing in the whole universe will be able to separate us from his love.'

Romans 8 supplies the answer to the question of chapter 7, ' Who shall deliver us from sin and death? ' ' God will,' Paul answers, ' through Christ. He has given his Son and the Holy Spirit to make it possible.' The general theme is life in the Spirit. Paul begins with an exposition of God's saving work in Christ and the Spirit (1-17), breaks into a prophetic soliloquy on his redemptive purpose in the travail of history (18-30), and climaxes in the conviction that nothing in the world or out of it shall be able to sunder us from God's love in Christ (31-39).

1-4. GOD'S SAVING ACT IN CHRIST

1. There is therefore now no condemnation to them that are in Christ Jesus

CONDEMNATION in plenty there had been in the opening chapters; but for those THAT ARE IN CHRIST JESUS—those who belong to the new divine community of which he is Head—the sentence of doom is lifted. The old 'order' (lit. 'law') of sin and death has been superseded by one of Spirit and life—life in Christ. The law of Moses, designed to give life, failed because it could not break the hold sin had got on us through our weak human nature. Now, what the law could not do, God has done, in another way. He has sent HIS OWN SON (the Son by nature, as we are sons by grace) IN THE LIKENESS OF SINFUL FLESH—in that nature which *in us* is infected by sin. The phrase implies a life incarnate but sinless. 'The flesh of Christ is "like" ours inasmuch as it is flesh: "like", and only "like", because it is not sinful.'[1]

More, God has sent his Son AS AN OFFERING FOR SIN. This phrase adds the atonement to the incarnation. The LXX's frequent use of *peri hamartias* (Paul's Greek here) to render the Hebrew for 'sin offering' makes the RV's AS AN OFFERING FOR SIN more likely than the AV's FOR SIN. So God CONDEMNED SIN IN THE FLESH. The phrase, which comes from the law-court, means that God (in the Cross?) passed effective sentence on sin in the sphere which it had claimed as its own—the flesh. God's purpose in this was that 'the just requirement of the law' (viz. a righteous life) might be fulfilled in us, inasmuch as we walk not by the

[1] Sanday and Headlam, *Romans, ad loc.*

flesh but by the Spirit.' Thus, with sin sentenced to death, and with the power which the Spirit supplies, we are now able to live as God wills that we should live. (What a weight of theology Paul packs into these first four verses!)

2. Put commas after SPIRIT and after JESUS, and this difficult verse becomes clearer. Paul means: 'The principle of the Spirit—i.e. of the life in Christ Jesus—has set me free.' He identifies *the Spirit* with the *life in Christ* (i.e. in the community of believers.)[1]

3. A broken construction, or *anacolouthon*, as the grammarians say. Paul begins his sentence in one way, and finishes it in another.

4. The ordinance of the law

Our old friend *dikaiōma* (Cf. 5.16 and 5.18) has here its commoner meaning of 'what is laid down as right' (Cf. 1.32 and 2.26) and so 'just requirement' (RSV).

5-11. LIFE IN THE SPIRIT

Two powers claim men for themselves, 'flesh' and 'Spirit'. 'Flesh' is our human nature as vitiated by sin. 'Spirit' is the divine supernatural power belonging to God's new order in Christ. All turns upon which of these two irreconcilable foes gains the upper hand in a man's life. Surrender to the flesh is the road to ruin: surrender to the Spirit the road to LIFE AND PEACE. Why is the way of the flesh fatal? Because the flesh, as the seat of indwelling sin, is in revolt against God, and those who take its way can never hope to please him. 'But,' says Paul addressing his readers, '*you* can please him, since as Christians you have God's Spirit in you. Not to have Christ's Spirit (clearly the same thing as God's) is not to belong to him.'

Then, in vv. 10-11, he explains the consequences of Christ's

[1] John Knox, *The Interpreter's Bible*, 9, 506.

indwelling of the Christian through the Spirit: life and immortality. The Christian's BODY, so far as it is in the flesh,
the seat of sin, experiences death; but his SPIRIT (the
human spirit) is alive BECAUSE OF RIGHTEOUSNESS, i.e. the
salvation it has found in Christ. And the future is assured:
the Spirit which indwells the Christian is that of God who
raised Christ, and as such it guarantees that our MORTAL
BODIES (as well as our spirits) will be quickened into
immortality. (What Paul means, he explains in I Cor. 15.)

9f. These verses enable us to make the following equation:
God's Spirit=Christ's Spirit=Christ in you. All describe
the same work of God in Christ. Paul finds it impossible
to distinguish between the work of God and the work of
Christ in a human soul, and like St. John he regards the
Holy Spirit as the *alter ego* of Christ.

12-17. SONS AND HEIRS

This hope, Paul says (12f.), lays us under obligation to
live the way life lies—in the Spirit. The natural man may
think that the way of the flesh is 'life'. Paul says it leads
to death. So Augustine, looking back on his life according
to the flesh, mused sadly: 'Such was my life—was that
life?'

Then (14ff.) he develops a new thought. Life in the Spirit
is the mark of those who are SONS OF GOD. 'Son' (*hyios*)
'suggests status and privilege as well as the natural relationship of a child' (*teknon*) (v. 16). They are *adopted* sons:
Paul uses the metaphor of adoption to signify that we are
by grace what Christ is by nature. And the Spirit which
informs them now is no craven fear—as of slaves before a
stern master—but one which unseals their lips in filial speech
to God.

WHEN WE CRY ABBA, FATHER, Paul says, THE SPIRIT HIM-
SELF BEARETH WITNESS WITH OUR SPIRIT, THAT WE ARE THE
CHILDREN OF GOD. We hear, as it were, two inner voices—

the Holy Spirit's and our own—assuring us that we are
God's children. The word both keep saying is ABBA, the
Aramaic word Christ had used in his prayer-speech (Mark
14.36). Hallowed by his usage, it had passed over into the
Greek-speaking Church where the word *patēr* was added to
interpret it (as in our hymn, ' Amen. So let it be.').

17. And if children, then heirs

As children of a household can look forward to heiring
their portion of their father's possessions, so Christians, as
sons of God, will one day enter on their heavenly inheritance, as their Elder Brother has already done. What is
Christ's now is reserved for those who are 'in Christ'. But
there is a condition attached: IF SO BE THAT WE SUFFER
WITH HIM. For Christ the path of suffering was the path
to glory. For his JOINT-HEIRS it must be the same.

15f. Adoption,

unknown in Jewish circles, was a familiar practice in the
Graeco-Roman world. A wealthy man who was childless
might adopt a slave youth into his family as his son. So,
in Christ, God admits us into his family circle.

It is probably best (with Moffatt and the RSV) to put a
period after ADOPTION, and take the last clause of v. 15
along with v. 16: 'When we cry Abba, Father, the Spirit
himself beareth witness with our spirit that we are children
of God.'

18-25. PRESENT PAINS AND FUTURE GLORY

Paul has just linked suffering and glory together; but, in
his judgment, THE SUFFERINGS OF THIS PRESENT TIME ARE
NOT WORTHY TO BE COMPARED WITH THE GLORY WHICH
SHALL BE REVEALED TO US. He is thinking of the Con-
summation of all things when God will complete his saving
purposes for man and the world. Then will come THE
REVEALING OF THE SONS OF GOD, an event for which he.

F

pictures the creation waiting with 'eager expectancy'. FOR
THE CREATION WAS SUBJECTED TO VANITY . . . IN HOPE. Ours
is a fallen world; all around we see evidences of waste and
futility; but these things are there by divine decree, BY
REASON OF HIM WHO SUBJECTED IT. The reference is to
God who, at the Fall, pronounced the sentence, CURSED IS
THE GROUND FOR THY SAKE (Gen. 3.17); but God also wills
that the curse shall be lifted. If the creation suffered with
man in his Fall, God means it also to share in his final
beatitude. THE BONDAGE OF CORRUPTION, the sad and
sombre appointing of all things to decay, will pass away
and be replaced by THE GLORIOUS LIBERTY OF THE CHILDREN
OF GOD (AV), a phrase suggesting the unimaginable freedom
and perfection of the final state of the redeemed.

Paul has noted the pathos and sorrow of nature. 'He
thinks,' says John Knox,[1] 'of the suffering of animals—the
weak devoured by the strong—of the ruthless destruction
of plant life, of natural catastrophes of all kinds; he listens
to the cryings of the wind and the sea.' THE WHOLE
CREATION GROANETH AND TRAVAILETH IN PAIN TOGETHER
UNTIL NOW is how he phrases it. The metaphor is from
child-birth. Like a woman in labour, the world is sighing
for release from agony; but 'it does so with hope for that
which will give meaning to all the pain and turn it into joy'.
This sighing is shared, Paul adds (v. 23), even by us Christians. We wait FOR OUR ADOPTION, the full and final divine
declaration of our sonship, and THE REDEMPTION OF OUR
BODY, that is, the complete deliverance of our personalities
from sin and death and their investiture with glory. In this
hope, Paul says, WE WERE SAVED (v. 24), and in this hope
we can bear all present pains with patience.

In this great passage, Paul stands revealed as a poet who
'hath kept watch o'er man's mortality'. He is no pessimist.
The travail of the ages is not in vain. Suffering has a purpose, and its end the:

[1] John Knox, *The Interpreter's Bible*, 521.

> *One far-off divine event*
> *To which the whole creation moves.*

Much of it has its roots in the Jewish apocalyptic hope which, basing itself on Isa. 65.17ff., painted glowing (and often garish) pictures of 'a new heaven and a new earth'. The faith behind this hope Paul shares; but in his own picture the crudities and exclusivisms disappear. Moreover, as a Christian, he knows that the glories of 'V-Day' (to borrow Cullmann's terms) will be simply an unfolding of the event of 'D-Day', when in the Cross and Resurrection God began the process of redemption yet to be completed.

Christians to-day are committed to this hope, but not necessarily to all Paul's details. Some may reject his belief in a final renovation of all nature, holding that the created world is but the stage-work for man's redemption which, having served its purpose, must fall away. Others will argue that the creation, once very good, must be restored to its primal perfection. All will unite in the conviction of St. Paul that the travail of history and the world have a divine meaning, and that all is moving to a God-appointed end.

19. Earnest expectation

The Greek word *apokaradokia* means literally 'watching with outstretched head'.

23. The first-fruits of the Spirit

The Christian's possession of the Holy Spirit is the pledge and first instalment of his heavenly inheritance. Elsewhere (II Cor. 1.22, 5.5 and Eph. 1.14) Paul calls the Spirit our *arrabōn* or 'guarantee'.

26-30. THE HELPING SPIRIT AND CHRISTIAN ASSURANCE

As hope sustains us, so does the Spirit help us in our weakness. When we falter in our prayers, the Holy Spirit, like some unseen friend, pleads our cause, and he 'unto

whom all hearts be open' understands these 'sighs too deep
for words' (RSV). The 'sighs' are no doubt those uttered
at church meetings under stress of deep religious emotion
(cf. I Cor. 14.13-19). What a profound doctrine of prayer
is here—'the divine within us appealing to the divine above
us'! And what comfort for the unready in prayer to know
that the Spirit is there to reinforce their soul's inarticulate
desires!

Paul adds (v. 28) yet another ground of confidence for the
future. God's elect may count on his co-operation for good
in all that befalls them. The familiar AV rendering ALL
THINGS WORK TOGETHER FOR GOOD should probably yield
to the RSV's 'In everything God works for good with those
who love him'. (This is to read *ho theos* 'God'—with
excellent support from the MSS—before *synergei* 'works
with', and to take *panta* as an accusative of respect.) The
new translation, besides making the divine help more personal, seems to fit Paul's thought better. In all circumstances—bitter not less than sweet—those who love God
may count on his working with them for their good. As
THEM THAT LOVE GOD describes believers subjectively, from
the human angle, so THEM THAT ARE CALLED ACCORDING TO
HIS PURPOSE describes them objectively, in their relation to
the will of God. Wilson of the Antarctic understood Paul
when he wrote in his diary:[1] 'This I know is God's own
truth, that pain and trouble and trials and sorrows and dis-
appointments are either one thing or another. To all men
who love God they are love tokens from him. To all who
do not love God and do not want to love him, they are
merely a nuisance.'

The thought of God's PURPOSE or plan moves Paul (v. 29)
to say a word about the believer's place in it. When, in
eternity, God FOREKNEW his own, i.e. took note of them for
a special purpose, he planned that they should BE CON-
FORMED TO THE IMAGE OF HIS SON—share the glorified body

[1] George Seaver, *Edward Wilson of the Antarctic*, 71.

of his risen Son—and so come to form a great family in which Christ, as first risen from the dead, ranks as Eldest Brother.

Having passed from the plan to the completed purpose—from eternity to eternity—Paul returns (v. 30) to the intermediate steps in time whereby God puts his plan into effect: first their *calling* by God; then, when they heard it (' calling ' in the New Testament is always ' effective calling') their *justification*, or acquittal; and finally—though this is a daring anticipation of faith—their *glorification*.

When Paul speaks here of predestination, he speaks as a saved man rather than as a dogmatic theologian. A man who has deeply known God's grace does not regard it as an accidental benefit on which he has stumbled; he comes to feel that, without any will or act of his own, God has eternally marked him out for salvation. So Paul felt. It is when we try to turn this religious experience of grace into a theological dogma that we land ourselves in the insoluble problems raised by divine sovereignty and human free-will. Here let us note that this very chapter which speaks of these things, contains also Paul's injunctions to *decide* between life and death (12ff.). Probably only a faith which proceeds from a very real sense of human responsibility has a right to believe in eternal election.

31-39. THE LOVE THAT DOES NOT LET GO

31. What shall we then say to these things?

These evidences of God's loving interest in his own? Paul answers his question with another: With God on our side, what does it matter who ranges himself against us? The God, who, like Abraham (Gen. 22.12), did not shrink from sacrificing his own Son for us, may be trusted to give us all we need. Thus, ' the Christian's faith in Providence is an inference from Redemption '.[1]

[1] Denney, *ad loc.*

But will not our sin separate us from God? This is the question underlying v. 33. In answer, Paul again borrows the language of the law-court. We may be like accused men in the dock. But who dare lay a charge against us when God the Judge pronounces our sentence of acquittal? WHO IS HE THAT SHALL CONDEMN? The only possible condemner is Christ; but he, so far from this, has done, and is doing, everything to save us. Having shed his blood for us, he now pleads our cause before the Throne. Truly the prosecutor has turned advocate for the defence!

But if sin cannot separate, suffering may (35). When Paul denies this, let us remember that he speaks of what he knows (see II Cor. 11.23ff.). Nor does he hide the fact that suffering is the Christian's lot. FOR THY SAKE (i.e. for Christ's) he says, quoting Ps. 44.22, WE ARE KILLED ALL THE DAY LONG, WE ARE ACCOUNTED AS SHEEP FOR THE SLAUGHTER. Nevertheless, whatever form the suffering may take—TRIBULATION, ANGUISH, PERSECUTION, FAMINE, NAKEDNESS, PERIL, THE SWORD—it cannot separate from the Divine Love in Christ. On the contrary, WE ARE MORE THAN CONQUERORS THROUGH HIM THAT LOVED *(agapēsantos)* US; the past tense of the participle 'loved' pointing back to Christ's death as the crowning proof of his love.

Finally, in 38, he gathers all up into his great conviction:

38. For I am persuaded
Having ruled out sin and suffering as possible separators, he now declares that nothing in the cosmos can sunder us from the Divine Love.

Neither death nor life
Nothing in death nor life.

Nor angels, nor principalities, nor powers:
No super-human beings nor spirit-powers.

Nor things present nor things to come:
   No terror that the present or the future may hold.

Nor height nor depth:
   No influence of the stars in their courses.

Nor any other creature:
   Better: 'nor anything else in creation'.

   So, in one last summarizing phrase, Paul sweeps all possible separators aside, asserting the utter adequacy of THE LOVE OF GOD IN CHRIST JESUS OUR LORD to hold us to the very end.

   The great argument of chapters 1-8 which, starting from the sin of man, went on to proclaim the grace of God in Christ, is over.   In 9-11 Paul will discuss the tragedy of Israel's rejection, and in 12-15 the Christian Ethic which flows from the gospel.

39. Nor height nor depth:
   The terms are probably astrological.   HEIGHT (*hypsōma*): the highest point a star reaches;   DEPTH (*bathos*), the abyss out of which it rises.   The position of the stars was supposed to affect human destinies.   'Whatever the stars may be supposed to do,' Paul says, 'they cannot separate us from God's love.

IX

PARAPHRASE

' *Believe me, my heart fills with sorrow at the fate of my Jewish kinsmen. When I consider Israel's unique privileges, I could even wish myself a lost soul, if that would mean their saving.*

Has then God's purpose gone awry? No, the Jewish nation as a whole was never able to claim the divine promises. Go back to the beginning, and you will note a process of selection at work. Of Abraham's sons, only Isaac is chosen; of Isaac's, only Jacob. If we ask why, the answer is that God is sovereign and acts as he deems fit. To queston his will is as absurd as for the pot to criticize the potter. Moreover, while some Jews have fallen out of his favour, God always purposed to include Gentiles in his people. This is happening now.

The position is this. Gentiles who did not make righteousness their quest, have found it—and found it by faith; whereas Israel, though it was all their aim, have missed it. Why? Because their method, works, was wrong.'

THE REJECTION OF THE JEWS
9-11

' He came to his own home, and his own people received him not ' (John 1.11). Why? This is the problem Paul wrestles with in chapters 9-11, which, structurally, seem to stand apart from the rest of the letter. Why have the Jews rejected the gospel? Have God's plans and promises for his people completely miscarried?

His solution proceeds along three lines. (1) God is sovereign, and may, if he so pleases, will the rejection of the

Jews (9.6-27); (2) if we consider it from the angle of human free-will, we may say that the Jews, by their own disobedience, have rejected themselves (9.30–10.21); but (3) ultimately, God's promises to Israel must be fulfilled, and Jew as well as Gentile find salvation (11.1-32).

1-5. PAUL'S GRIEF FOR APOSTATE ISRAEL

1-3. The verses which introduce this section voice Paul's sorrow at the apparent rejection of his people. To save them, he is willing to become ANATHEMA FROM CHRIST (the Greek word corresponds to the Hebrew *hĕrĕm*, which means something put to the ban and irrevocably devoted to destruction). We think of Moses' cry in like circumstances, 'Yet now, if thou wilt, forgive their sin; but if not, blot me, I pray thee, out of the book which thou hast written' (Ex. 32.32). Moses would perish *with* his people, if they cannot be saved. Paul can find it in his heart to perish *for* them. The cry 'is a spark from the fire of Christ's substitutionary love' (Dorner).

4f. With mournful pride Paul lists the privileges of Israel as the elect people: ISRAELITES: the theocratic name (Gen. 32.28); THE ADOPTION: i.e. of Israel as God's son (Ex. 4.22, ISRAEL IS MY SON, MY FIRST-BORN); THE GLORY: the glorious presence of God among his people (Ex. 16.10); THE COVENANTS: with Abraham, etc; THE GIVING OF THE LAW: at Sinai; THE SERVICE OF GOD: the Temple worship; THE PROMISES: of the Messiah and the Kingdom; THE FATHERS: the Jewish patriarchs: Abraham, Isaac and Jacob. The catalogue ends with Jesus the Messiah who, so far as natural descent goes, has been born a Jew. But what are we to make of the words WHO IS OVER ALL GOD BLESSED FOR EVER? Both AV and RV refer them to Christ. So did the fathers of the Church and so do some moderns. (Even Socinus, no champion of Christ's deity, owned this was the natural interpretation.) But most recent commentators, including the makers of the RSV, put a full-stop after THE FLESH and take the remaining words as a doxology addressed to God: 'God who is over all be blessed for ever.' They do so for two reasons: (1) the pattern of Paul's other doxologies—e.g. Rom. 1.25 and 11.36, and (2) the fact that elsewhere Paul seems to stop short of calling Christ 'God'.

6-29. GOD'S SOVEREIGN PURPOSE

Some of Paul's language about the divine sovereignty in this section (see especially vv. 18 and 20) will move most of us to dissent. But if Paul overstresses the divine sovereignty, do not most of us go to the opposite extreme, making of God a kind of honorary President of the universe, who can, for all practical purposes, be ignored?

It will conduce to clearness if we split the section up into three parts:

6-13. GOD CHOOSES AS HE WILLS.
14-21. MAN HAS NO RIGHT TO CAVIL.
22-29. GOD IS VERY PATIENT, AND HIS PLAN IS TO BE JUDGED BY ITS POSITIVE RESULTS.

6-13. It is wrong (Paul argues) to suppose God's purpose has miscarried. What we are seeing now is a divine way of working traceable in Israel's history from the beginning. Not all 'Israelites' belong to the Israel of God; it has never been so—God has never made bodily descent the title to a place in his family. Consider the story of the patriarchs. Of Abraham's two sons, God chose Isaac to carry forward his saving purpose. Isaac was born to Abraham following a divine promise, and was not merely, like Ishmael, a child of the flesh. God's true children are always of this kind. You may see the same thing happening in the next generation. Isaac's wife, Rebecca, conceived twin sons, Esau and

Jacob. Before their birth—before they had done anything creditable or discreditable—God's choice fell on the younger, Jacob. So God selected long ago; so he is selecting still.

Paul uses four quotations from the OT here. The first in v. 7 is from Gen. 21.12, the second in v. 9 from Gen. 18.10, the third in v. 12 from Gen. 25.23, and the fourth in v. 13 from Mal. 1.2, 3. The point of the words NEITHER HAVING DONE ANYTHING GOOD OR BAD is that claims as of right on God, whether based on birth or on works, are futile.

14-21. If God chooses as he pleases (somebody may object) he cannot act fairly. Paul repudiates the objection. God himself says he saves in this way, and the way God calls his own cannot be unjust. Thus everything depends not on man's will or effort but on God's mercy. (Paul could have stopped here—at v. 16. He did not need to drag in Pharaoh as an example of 'the shadow side' of God's sovereignty. But he continues.) Take the case of Pharaoh. God raised up that bad man simply to show his power. Thus, whether he saves or judges, God acts as he wills. The objector may protest: 'If God decrees that men should act like Pharaoh, he cannot condemn them for doing so.' The objection is unanswerable, and Paul merely repels it. Man, he says, has no more right to talk back to his Creator than the pot to the potter. (Here we dissent emphatically. For 'man is not a pot. He will ask, Why did you make me thus? And he will not be silenced.'[1])

15. Ex. 33.19.

17. Ex. 9.16. In Pharaoh's case God 'showed his power' in the penal miracles preceding the Exodus.

18. The logic of this verse is that we are simply puppets

[1] Dodd, *Romans*, *ad loc.*

controlled by a cruelly capricious God like Hardy's 'President of the Immortals'.

20. For the imagery see Isa. 29.16 and 45.9f.

22-29. Paul's argument has really reached an *impasse*, but he tries to evade it.

The thought of vv. 22-24 seems to be this: 'God acts with sovereign freedom, but he is not a non-moral despot, for (1) although some are objects of his wrath and ripe for doom, these very men he treats with great patience; and (2) his plan should be judged not by its negative results, viz. in excluding some men, but by its positive ones, viz. in bringing blessings to the chosen. And that means ourselves, Gentiles as well as Jews.'

22. The *protasis* (or 'if' clause) implies some such *apodosis* as, 'Who dare find fault?'

25f. This exposition of God's ways with men is congruent with his words in scripture, as witness Hos. 2.23 and 1.10. The words Paul applies to the calling of the Gentiles referred originally to the restoration of Israel.

27. Isa. 10.22f. Isaiah's doctrine of the faithful remnant applied to the Church. Only a minority of historic Israel, said Isaiah, would be saved. This has proved true.

29. Isa. 1.9.

30-33. THE CAUSE OF ISRAEL'S FAILURE

These verses introduce the theme developed in chapter 10. There Paul will show that the Jews have, in a sense, rejected themselves. Persisting in a path where righteousness was not to be found, they have landed in a *cul-de-sac*. Paradoxical as it may sound, this agrees with scripture's words about a stone of stumbling.

Paul puts together two passages from Isaiah—28.16 and 8.14—which tell of a stumbling stone. The stone in Paul's mind is, of course, Jesus the Messiah whom the Jews have rejected. Since these same two passages are combined in I Pet. 2.6-8, we may guess that the apostolic preachers, following their Lord (see Mark 12.10), dwelt often (no doubt in controversy with the Jews) on the 'stoneship' of Christ.

X

'My heart's desire is for the salvation of my people. But, alas, they go the wrong way about it—they want to save themselves, by works. Faith is the true way, and the gospel, so far from being difficult, is really very simple. Confess "Jesus is Lord" and believe that he is risen—that is the heart of it.

But the Jews never had a chance of accepting Christ? Of course they had! The gospel heralds have gone everywhere—you cannot put down Israel's failure to ignorance. No more can you attribute it to lack of understanding. Why, their own prophets predicted not only that Israel would prove disobedient, but that others, apparently beyond the pale of God's mercy, would find it.'

1-13. HOW ISRAEL HAS GONE ASTRAY

'The Jews,' Paul says, 'whose salvation is my dearest desire, for all their earnestness about religion, are misguided: instead of accepting salvation as God's gift, they want to save themselves, by works—to earn their way into God's favour. In vain! With Christ in the field, the day of legal religion is done.

There are two ways of getting right with God—the way of Moses (law) and the way of Christ (faith). The first says: the way is by a *tour de force* of works of law. The other says: no such *tour de force* is necessary: you need neither scale the heights of heaven nor descend into the underworld. All you need to do is to accept Christ—who is here and waiting for you—as your Saviour. Confess him as Lord and believe he has conquered death—that is enough. Such faith saves, as the scripture says. And not only is salvation easily

94

accessible; it is universal, with Jew and Gentile on the same footing.'

Behind these verses it is not hard to discern Paul's own struggle to find salvation. The way of Moses—how long and earnestly he had sought righteousness along that road! He had not found it. Instead there had followed defeat and despair, with all the spiritual agonies of a man consumed by a 'zeal for God', yet seemingly fated for ever to miss that peace with God for which he longed. Then came the decisive encounter with the living Christ on the Damascus Road, defeat was turned into victory, and O WRETCHED MAN THAT I AM became I CAN DO ALL THINGS IN HIM WHO STRENGTHENS ME.

Salvation is not a matter of achieving but of believing. We receive it—at Christ's hands; we do not earn it. No heroic attempts to storm the citadel of heaven or the kingdom of the dead are needed. Christ the Saviour is here, incarnate and risen, God's gift to every man with faith, be he Jew or Gentile. Whittier has put it in lovely verse:

> *We may not climb the heavenly steeps*
> *To bring the Lord Christ down;*
> *In vain we search the lowest deeps,*
> *For him no depths can drown.*

> *And warm, sweet, tender, even yet*
> *A present help is he;*
> *And faith has still its Olivet*
> *And love its Galilee.*

3. Seeking to establish their own

The Jews tried to 'be good men without becoming God's debtors'. Some Christians are still like that.

4. Christ is the end of the law

End (*telos*) means terminus. With Christ in the field, law as a way of salvation is finished.

5. Moses writeth:
Lev. 18.5.

6-9. To show the difference between righteousness-by-the-law and righteousness-by-faith, Paul adopts words from Deut. 30.12-14—words originally referring to the law. Paul's meaning is: no impossible preliminaries are necessary before true religion is got under way. In v. 9 the true text is probably, 'if you confess with your lips that Jesus is Lord'. This was the earliest Christian confession of faith (see I Cor. 12.3 and Phil. 2.11), and when the Christians made it, they were not merely conferring an honorific title on Jesus, they were affirming that Jesus now reigned in grace over both the Church and the world. To say *Kyrios Jesus* is to say *Christus regnat*—to assert 'the crown rights of the Redeemer'.

Believe that God raised him from the dead

The Cross is central to St. Paul? Of course it is, but we do not always remember that the Resurrection is equally central, and that 'the strange man on his cross' cannot save us unless he be also the risen and ever-living One. (I have heard a venerable and eloquent Scottish divine, on Easter Day, exhorting, at great length, candidates for the Ministry to 'preach the Cross' without so much as one passing reference to the Resurrection.) 'To be a Christian is to have a risen Lord, and through him to share in his resurrection life' (Nygren).[1]

10. The contrast between HEART and MOUTH is merely rhetorical: a heart believing unto righteousness and a mouth confessing unto salvation are two sides of one medal.

11. Isa. 28.16, already quoted in 9.33.

---

[1] *Romans, ad loc.*

12. As in sin, so also in salvation: Jew and Greek are on the same level, for Christ is the gracious Saviour of both.

13. Joel 2.32. In the OT THE LORD is Jehovah. That Paul can apply this scripture to Christ, shows how completely, for him, he stands on the divine side of reality.

14-21. THE DISOBEDIENCE OF ISRAEL

The sum of Paul's argument here is: Israel's downfall is due not to ignorance, or to lack of understanding, but to sheer disobedience.

What is the point of the four questions at the beginning? The plea might be advanced that, in fact, Israel had never had a fair chance of hearing the gospel. To rebut it, Paul begins by asking, What conditions must be fulfilled before a man can call on Christ as Saviour? The answer (implied in the questions) is: first, a preacher, sent by God; then, a gospel for him to proclaim; and finally, a man to hear that gospel and believe it. In Israel's case, these conditions have been fulfilled; yet they have not believed. Why? Because they never got a proper chance of hearing the gospel preached? This is absurd, Paul says, for the gospel heralds went everywhere. Because they did not understand, then? No, the fact is that others (the Gentiles) one would never have expected, have found salvation, whereas Israel, true to form—witness the scriptures—proved a stubborn and unresponsive people. In short, crass disobedience has caused Israel's downfall.

Paul's argument is borne along on OT quotations. In v. 15 he quotes Isa. 52.7, following it in v. 16 with Isa. 53.1. In v. 18 instead of citing the wide-spread activity of the Christian missionaries, he quotes Ps. 19.4 (which referred originally to the sun and the heavenly bodies). Then in v. 19 we have Deut. 32.21, followed in vv. 20 and 21 by Isa. 65.1 and 65.2.

We cannot help asking, Why do so many of our own

G

people to-day reject the gospel? We too may reply with Paul, that it is not because they have never had the chance of hearing it. Nor are they to be excused on the ground that they do not understand it, when preaching from pulpit and radio has made its essential content plain to the humblest intellect. Is the cause just sheer apathy and indifference? Is it that we Christians are very unattractive advertisements for our faith? Or is it that to many of the men of to-day, Christ is still what he was to the Jews, a stumbling-block? Do they find it hard to see, in a man who was hanged, the master-clue to the riddle of the world?

XI

PARAPHRASE

' But God has not really repudiated his people. Now, as in Elijah's day, God of his grace has chosen a faithful remnant. The rest of Israel remains in a state of stupor which prevents their seeing or hearing properly. But their lapse from grace is not final and has meant the salvation of the Gentiles. What wealth is in prospect when Israel shall be completely restored!

My apostolic zeal among you Gentiles is meant to stir my own countrymen to jealousy and so save some, for Israel remains precious and holy in God's sight.

Think of Israel as an olive tree, of which the patriarchs form the root. The unbelieving Jews are branches broken off it for their unfaithfulness. You Gentiles are wild shoots grafted into it. I find here both a warning and a hope. The warning concerns you Gentiles—be humble, or you may forfeit your high privilege. The hope is for the Jews: if they repent, they can be re-ingrafted.

I will let you into a divine secret. This ' hardening' of Israel will not be permanent. It will last only till the mass of Gentiles comes in. Just as you Gentiles, once disobedient, have found God's mercy, so it will be with the Jews. Universal disobedience is to issue in universal salvation. How incomparably wise God is!

We reach the third stage in Paul's ' theodicy '. In chapter 9 he argues: ' God is sovereign, and elects whom he wills.' In chapter 10 he says: ' This is not the whole truth. God's judgment on Israel is not arbitrary, for in fact the Jews' own disobedience led to their downfall.' But he cannot rest in this sad conclusion, and therefore in chapter 11 he goes on to say, 'This is not God's last word. Israel is not doomed to final rejection. Her temporary lapse forms part of God's great plan. Through Israel's lapse the Gentiles have found salvation. And Gentile acceptance of the gospel is meant so to move the Jews to jealousy (at seeing their own promised blessings in Gentile hands) that they will ultimately accept what they now reject. And so all Israel will be saved.'

1-12. THE ELECT REMNANT

1f. As a good Jew, Paul recoils in horror from the very suggestion that God has repudiated his own people. What is happening now happened long ago—in Elijah's day. When the picture seemed to the prophet one of complete apostasy, God showed him 7,000 loyal souls who had resisted Baal's seductions. History is repeating itself in the present situation, Paul says. The small body of Jewish Christians corresponds to the loyal 7,000—they form the faithful remnant. (When we speak of the doctrine of the remnant, Nygren's words[1] are worth remembering: 'A remnant is not just a group of separate individuals, taken out of a people doomed to overthrow. It is itself the chosen people; it is Israel *in nuce*. It is the seed which, after the winter, will bear the harvest. In the remnant, Israel lives on as the People of God.')

7ff. How shall we describe the condition of the remaining Jews? Paul finds two metaphors: (1) 'hardening' (*pōrōsis*)—it is as if a callus had grown over their spiritual heart making them impervious to new truth; and (2) 'sleepy-headedness' (Isa. 29.10)—it is as if a drowsy stupor had dulled their spiritual faculties. To these metaphors he adds scripture words from Isa. 29.10 and Ps. 69.22f.

---

[1] *Romans, ad loc.*

11f. But Paul cannot believe that his nation is 'out for the count', as we say. It will rise again, and if its fall has brought blessing to the Gentile world, what wealth is in store when 'the full inclusion' of Israel takes place!

2. Elijah
I Kings 19.10.

4. The answer of God
I Kings 19.18.

6. These Jewish Christians, who form the remnant, have not earned their election. It is a matter of pure grace, for 'Grace', as Augustine said, 'unless it is gratis, is not grace'.

11. To provoke them to jealousy
The very sight of Gentiles among God's chosen people will stir the apostate Jews to a saving envy.

13-24. THE INGRAFTING OF ISRAEL
Paul has been using the doctrine of the remnant to illuminate the mystery of Israel's rejection. Now he develops the theme of vv. 11 and 12. Israel's fall is to be, under God, not an end but a means—a means to the saving of the Gentiles. Not only so, but beyond the saving of the Gentiles shines the hope of the conversion of Israel herself.

13ff. He turns to the Gentile Christians. His own zeal among them is motivated by the hope that he may thus move his own fellow-countrymen to envy and convert some of them. So, indirectly, the apostle to the Gentiles may prove an apostle to Israel. V. 15 reaffirms the glorious prospect of v. 12. In prophetic vision Paul sees the home-coming of the Jews. What a great day for humanity that will be! It will be LIFE FROM THE DEAD—like a father welcoming back his prodigal son whom he had given up as dead. (Cf. Luke 15.24. God looking on Israel will say, 'This my son was dead and is alive again. He was lost, and is found.')

16ff. Nor is this merely a wild dream. Long ago God chose Israel from the nations, and Israel remains still the object of his favour. To make his point, Paul employs two figures: THE FIRST-FRUITS and THE OLIVE TREE. For light on the first we turn to Num. 15.19-21. The offering to God, as first-fruits, of a cake of meal, was deemed to sanctify the whole mass of dough, and indeed the whole produce of the land. The figure of the root and the branches makes the same point. If God has chosen Israel as a precious tree, the holiness belonging to the root is shared by the branches. By 'first-fruits' and 'root' Paul means the patriarchs. And his point is that as the fathers, because chosen by God, were holy, that holiness belongs inalienably to Israel to this very day.

The second figure moves Paul to develop the allegory of the olive tree. The olive tree is the people of God. The native branches are the Jews, the wild shoots the Gentiles. The rich root signifies the patriarchs. (Nothing could better show the continuity between the Church of Christ and ancient Israel. The Holy Catholic Church is not a new society which came into the existence about A.D. 30. It is the legitimate continuation of the old People of God.)

With this key it is easy to understand the allegory. SOME OF THE BRANCHES WERE BROKEN OFF: God's judgment has excluded some Jews for their faithlessness. A WILD OLIVE WAS GRAFTED IN: God's grace has elected believing Gentiles to a place among God's people, with all the benefits derived from the rich ROOT, i.e., the wealth of divine blessings bestowed on the patriarchs. *N.B.* Grafting wild shoots on to a cultivated stock is the very reverse of what is done in the best gardening circles. No matter: if Paul's literary horticulture is faulty, his meaning is clear enough.

18ff. He addresses the Gentile Christians. First, he says, ' no glorying over the branches '—no crowing over fallen Israel. Why? Because every spiritual blessing you enjoy you owe to your connection with her. Second, if you are tempted to think, ' Since God has taken all this trouble over me, I must be very precious to him ', remember this—your faith alone keeps you where you are. So cultivate humility —a lively sense of awe at God's goodness to you—otherwise the same fate will befall you as has befallen the Jews.

22. Behold the goodness and severity of God

In other words, God is a God of grace but he is not to be paltered with, as the Jews know to their cost. Let the Gentiles beware of tasting that same severity! (We too may learn here. Any truly Christian doctrine of God must hold together the truths suggested by Paul's two abstract nouns. Neglect his SEVERITY, and we make of the Supreme Being a weak-kneed Benevolence. Ignore his GOODNESS, and we turn the gracious Father of Christ into a ruthless Omnipotence.)

We boggled at some of Paul's predestination language in chapter 9; but how little metaphysical it really is, appears here. The Gentiles have been elected, Paul says, yet they can as easily be rejected, if they do not CONTINUE IN HIS GOODNESS, i.e. continue in faith.

Finally, let the Gentiles never forget that there is hope for renegade Israel. AND THEY ALSO IF THEY CONTINUE NOT IN THEIR UNBELIEF, SHALL BE GRAFTED IN. Let the Jews only stop disbelieving and they may regain their ancient place in God's People. God can put them back there—yes, and even more easily than he can give the Gentiles a share in his kingdom.

The way is clear for Paul's last word on the subject.

25-36. GOD'S UNIVERSAL PURPOSE OF MERCY

25-27. To deliver the Gentiles from self-conceit, Paul now lets them into a MYSTERY, i.e. a secret truth about God's saving purpose disclosed not by argument but by revelation. The hardening of a part of Israel is to last only till the Gentile world as a whole enters the Church. AND SO— moved by saving envy of the Gentiles' happy lot—Israel as a whole shall be saved. Hitherto this had been hardly more than a pious hope. Now Paul declares it to belong to God's secret purpose, a purpose shadowed forth long ago in Isaiah.

28-32. As regards THE GOSPEL—the principles by which God gives the gospel to the world—the Jews are presently being treated as ENEMIES, so that the Gentiles may find their way into the kingdom. But this does not affect God's principle of election which makes the Jews ' dear ' to God for the sake of the patriarchs. The gift of his favour, once made, God will not take back. (' God never goes back on his gifts and call '—Moffatt.) Thus a parallelism can be traced in the destinies of both Gentiles and Jews. In both (though not at the same time) a day of disobedience is suc- ceeded by a day of mercy. The disobedience of the Gentiles ended when God, in his mercy, offered them the gospel, and they accepted it. Then it was Israel's turn to be disobedient. But for Israel too will dawn the day of mercy. God has shut up all, first Gentiles and then Jews, in the prison of disobedi- ence, that in the end he may show mercy to all.

Is Paul then a ' universalist '? May we hail him as a champion of what is called ' the Larger Hope '? Does Paul believe that, in the end, God will save every individual, however much he has sinned? We may well doubt it. In this passage he is clearly thinking in terms of races, not individuals. Moreover, elsewhere he clearly envisages the possibility of men ' perishing '.

33-36. Paul has reached the climax of his argument. On Israel's dark way, over which lay the shadows of guilt and 'hardening', has fallen the bright vision of God's ultimate mercy. The very thought of the glorious End, to which the divine purpose is moving through all the dialectic of history, leaves Paul 'lost in wonder, love and praise', and he unburdens his soul in a great doxology of gratitude.

26f. Isa. 59.20 and 27.9.

34f. Isa. 40.13 and Job 41.11.

36. 'All comes from him, all lives by him, all ends in him' (Moffatt). Probably a Hellenistic formula derived from Stoicism. But Paul never construed it like a Stoic. Between Paul's thought of God and the pantheistic conception of the Stoic lies a whole world of difference.

XII

THEREFORE THE CHRISTIAN ETHIC
12.1–15.13

'The gospel,' as the coloured man is reported to have said, 'has two sides—a believing side and a behaving side.' The closing chapters of Paul's letter deal with 'the behaving side'. We are now shown how the man who has experienced God's salvation ought to live in the new era which has come with the coming of Christ. The life has two marks: it is, first, a life 'in Christ', that is, in Christ's community, the Church; and it is, second, a life in 'love'.

How then shall we characterize the Christian ethic as Paul understands it?

First, it is not a systematic ethic of the kind we associate with the Greek moralists. Paul does not discuss the concept of 'duty', or descant on the *summum bonum*, or draw up lists of cardinal virtues.

Second, it is not a legalistic ethic on the Jewish pattern. Paul does not compile a code of regulations, and say, 'Keep these, and you will win God's approval'. If the Jewish legalist said, in effect, 'Do these, and you will live', Paul says rather, 'Live, and do these'.

For, third, Paul's ethic is a *gospel* ethic, in the sense that it grows out of, and is determined by the gospel. The gospel is the divine indicative which says: 'God loved you, a sinner, in Christ.' The ethic is the divine imperative based on that divine indicative, and it says: 'Therefore you must love one another.' Christian conduct, in Paul's view, should be the saved man's response in life and behaviour to God's mercy in Christ. 'I beseech you therefore by the mercies of God to present your bodies as a living sacrifice, holy and acceptable to God, which is your spiritual worship."

Fourth, the Christian ethic as Paul understood it is emphatically a *corporate* ethic. He thinks of the Christian, not as an isolated individual handling moral issues which concern himself primarily, but as one who is first and foremost a member of a divine community with clear responsibilities to his brother members. And what he is constantly saying (see, for example, Rom. 14) is, 'Act always as members of Christ's Body'.

Finally and generally, the Christian life is a life lived not under the slavery of written statutes, but under the inspiration of God's Holy Spirit which belongs to all who are 'in Christ'.

What then of the ethical precepts which fill chapters 12 and 13? We view these rightly, if we see in them Paul's attempt to sketch a general pattern for Christian living—'a compass rather than an ordnance map, direction rather than directions'.

In this pattern we may note two things which the commentary will amplify: (1) Paul's pattern for Christian behaviour owes much to Christ's. Again and again we shall light on echoes of *verba Christi*—those sayings of Jesus, preserved for us in the Gospels, in which he had given his disciples a pattern for living in the Kingdom of God. (2) It is perhaps the same point in another form when we say that the dominant motif of Paul's ethic is *agapē*, or Christian 'love': for Paul, following his Lord, makes love the masterkey of morals: not merely the first among a series of admirable moral qualities but the one which includes all the rest.

PARAPHRASE

*'To these divine mercies, then, the only proper response is
the dedication of all our faculties to God.*

*Don't be conceited. Let each use his particular gift as a
true member of Christ's Body. See that your love is genuine.
Be zealous, aglow in the Spirit, radiantly hopeful, steadfast
when trials come, constant in prayer and open-handed to
the needy. Bless your persecutors. Never pay back evil for
evil, but always try to keep the peace, leaving retribution to
God. Overcome evil by good.'*

1-2. THE RESPONSE OF THE REDEEMED

Having in chapters 1-8 rehearsed God's mercies to sinful
men in Christ (9-11 being a kind of 'insert', perhaps in-
dependently composed), Paul now shows what the response
of the redeemed should be—nothing less than the offering of
their BODIES—all their faculties, as we might say—to the
redeeming God. This SACRIFICE of theirs, in contrast to the
dead animals offered by Jews and pagans, should be one of
LIVING personalities. Such SERVICE (or 'worship') he describes as REASONABLE or (better) 'spiritual': it is the
worship appropriate to their new spiritual life. What Paul
desiderates is complete moral and mental transformation.
Though they still live in the *milieu* of the old world, they
are men of the new age, and must behave accordingly.
'Don't,' he counsels them, 'let the present world squeeze
you into its mould, but let God remould your minds from
within.' (It is often observed that Paul has little to say
about 'repentance'. Yet what is this but a summons to it?)
Given this spiritual transformation, they will PROVE—know
surely—what the good will of God is.

1. Reasonable

Tr. 'spiritual'. Hellenistic mystics in Paul's day used the
Greek word *logikos* to describe 'spiritual' sacrifice in contrast to animal sacrifice. Paul is thinking of the Christian's
offering of his life as informed by the Spirit.

3-8. CORPUS CHRISTI CONDUCT

Paul's ethics, we saw, are Corpus Christi ethics. (The theme of vv. 4-6 is expanded in I Cor. 12.12-30.) Now, when Paul speaks thus of the Body and its members, it is for him no mere figure of speech but a spiritual reality. We really *are* one Body (he means)—one great spiritual organism in which Christ is Head—and we really *are* members in our mutual relations. But if there is one-ness in Christ, that does not abolish manifoldness and difference.

What then? The first thing to be said is: ' No exaggerated notions of your own importance, please! Remember, if by God's grace you belong to Christ's Body, you are only one among many members. Each has his separate gift. Each needs the other.'

This caveat uttered, Paul bids each member exercise his particular gift (Gr. *charisma*, lit. " grace-gift ': the divine endowment for a specific task conferred on a Christian by God's Spirit). Seven of these gifts he lists: PROPHECY (inspired preaching), SERVICE (' social service ' we would call it), TEACHING (instruction in the faith), EXHORTATION (' pastoral counselling '?), giving (Christian LIBERALITY), ruling (administration), and showing MERCY (sick-visitation). *N.B.* There is nothing ' official ' here: all ministry is a function of membership in the Body, and each Christian has the function of ministry in some degree.

Whatever gift God gives you, Paul says, use it wholeheartedly. Is your gift for inspirational preaching?—do it with all the conviction God gives you. Is it for social service?—go to it with enthusiasm. It is for teaching?— then devote yourself to it. Is it for administration?—apply yourself with vigour. Is it for sick-visitation?—then do it radiantly.

It is still to-day no small Christian wisdom to know what your particular gift is, and to use it to the full. instead of tackling everything as though you had all the gifts.

9-21. THE WAY OF AGAPĒ

The first word of this section and the key-word of the whole is *agapē*. 'Charity', which once served as a translation, has come down in the world of words. 'Love' is better, though even it carries erotic and sentimental associations, covering as it does nowadays almost 'everything from Hollywood to heaven'. If we keep it as a translation, let us remember that *agapē* is essentially 'self-giving love' (in contrast to *erōs* which is 'desire') and that 'caring' is often our best English equivalent. This *agapē*, which in man represents the reflex of the divine love shown to us in Christ, is to be the Christian's rule of life in his relations with his fellow-men. For the rest, the necessity, the nature and the never-failingness of love are imperishably depicted in I Cor. 13, to which these verses in Romans correspond.

What are the features of true *agapē*? These: hatred of evil, brotherly kindness, fine courtesy, fervour, devotion, a radiant hope, fortitude in suffering, constancy in prayer, and open-handed hospitality. How does this 'love' express itself? It blesses its persecutors, sympathizes with men in their joys and sorrows, is never snobbish, nourishes no malice. Slow to disturb the peace, it leaves vengeance to God, and by active kindness to a foe disarms him in shame. Always its aim is to defeat evil by good.

How nobly reminiscent all this is not only of the spirit but even of the letter of the Sermon on the Mount! BLESS THEM THAT PERSECUTE YOU: CONDESCEND TO THINGS THAT ARE LOWLY (or perhaps: 'associate with the lowly'): RENDER TO NO MAN EVIL FOR EVIL: LIVE PEACEABLY WITH ALL MEN: AVENGE NOT YOURSELVES: OVERCOME EVIL WITH GOOD (Cf. Matt. 5.39, 44f., Mark 9.50, etc.). A moral teacher who gives these advices may surely claim, WE HAVE THE MIND OF CHRIST (I Cor. 2.16).

17. Take thought:
Prov. 3.4 (LXX).

19. Give place unto wrath

Lit. 'the wrath', i.e. God's. Not 'Let God deal with the man—his vengeance will be worse than any you can inflict', but 'Stand back, and let God punish him, if he so wills'. VENGEANCE IS MINE: Deut. 32.35.

20. A fine verse from Prov. 25.21, 22. FEED HIM. 'The New Testament never forgets the practical truth that spiritual fare is poor sustenance for an empty stomach.' The COALS OF FIRE are pangs of burning shame. Such kindness to an enemy will overwhelm him with remorse.

21. With this compare the command of Mattathias to his sons, 'Pay back the heathen for what they have done' (I Mac. 2.67f.).

XIII

PARAPHRASE

'*I bid you obey the civil powers as ordained by God. Though the good man need not fear, the bad man may well hold them in terror, for they execute God's justice on wrongdoing. And be sure to pay your taxes and other lawful debts.*

One debt the Christian never may discharge—the debt of love. Love truly, and you fulfil all the commandments.

The dawn of God's new day is breaking. So, remembering the time, be wakeful. It is our duty to array ourselves as children of the dawn. Therefore off with the old habits, and on with the habits befitting a soldier of Christ.'

1-7. THE CHRISTIAN AND THE STATE

When Paul was writing, the temporal rulers were all pagans, so that Christians must sometimes have been tempted, as subjects of 'King Jesus', to refuse the civil authorities obedience altogether. Perhaps this temper was prevalent in the Church in Rome, Christians arguing that pagan rulers had no jurisdiction over the 'sons' of God who were 'free' (Matt. 17.26).

1-4. In that case, what a rude shock vv. 1-7 must have given them! For Paul bluntly bids Christians accept the State (the existing one with all its faults, not some ideal one) as something which exists by God's appointing. Rebellion against the civil power is rebellion against God, and will lead to punishment. The State menaces only the malefactor, and the way to avoid its menace is well-doing. For the State, in the order of Providence, is a servant OF GOD, promoting good and punishing evil. The law-breaker

experiences its TERROR when it uses the sword of justice to
do God's work—his ' alien ' work no doubt (as Luther would
say) but still his work—for it is God who sets the sword in
the civil magistrate's hand.

5-7. Obedience to the civil power, then, has good theological
warrant, and the Christian who obeys should do so not
merely from fear of punishment but FOR CONSCIENCE SAKE,
because he knows God has conferred such authority on it.
Moreover, in such authority resides not only the State's right
to levy taxes from him, but also its rightful claim to the
respect of Christian men.

Paul's championship of the ' divine right ' of the State is
so strong that we naturally ask: Is his teaching biassed by
the fact that Roman power had helped and protected him,
a Roman citizen and proud of it? There may be truth in
this; nonetheless, it was one of Paul's firm convictions that
government is no arbitrary invention of man but an ordinance of God. He believed that ' the State is a part of the
natural moral order, and of divine appointment, but lying
outside the order of grace revealed in Christ '.[1]

Of course, Paul realized that the State can be the foe of
the good man as well as the bad. Was it not the Roman
State who, through its agent Pontius Pilate, had crucified the
Lord? Further, as Rom. 8.35f. shows, Paul expected the
Church to suffer 'persecution' and 'the sword'. Yet the
stubborn fact remains that the man who wrote Rom. 8.35f.
wrote also Rom. 13.4. The possibility of a persecuting State
did not shake his conviction that civil government is of
God's appointing.

Rom. 13 teaches therefore that in this present age the
State has a divinely decreed function. But this is not the
whole truth as Paul understands it. Elsewhere he sees that
Christians, as men of the new age, possessing ' a capital
city in heaven ', may in some measure stand aloof from

[1] Dodd, *Romans, ad loc.*

the earthly state.   Nor must we forget I Cor. 6 where Paul
rebukes the Corinthian Christians for taking their legal
disputes before pagan law-courts.

How does all this help our Christian thinking to-day?
The answer is that, while a Christian doctrine of the State
may well start from Rom. 13, it cannot stop there.   Modern
history confronts us with problems for answers to which we
look in vain to St. Paul.   Nevertheless, these verses may give
us food for thought.   For example, does the mere possession
of administrative power deserve the name of 'government'
in Christian eyes?   Certainly it is better than political chaos.
But the Christian cannot rest there.   He must insist that
such power be at the service of a constitution which recognizes the fundamentals of the moral law.   Again, have the
Christian subjects of a land the right, when faced with a
hopelessly corrupt government and all other remedies have
failed, to use force to set up a better political order?   This
question is not to be ruled out of court merely by quoting
Rom. 13.   What Paul condemns in these verses is rebellion
in the name of Christian freedom.   On the other hand, as a
descendant of the Maccabees, Paul surely knew that circumstances may arise when the man of faith must say an
absolute and passionate 'No' to the demands of the State.
In short, we must never employ Rom. 13 to justify an un-
conditional loyalty to the State which forgets that the
authority of God not only establishes the State and the
citizen's responsibility to it, but just as surely sets limits to
them both.

4. The sword
carried before the civil magistrate symbolized his power of
life and death.

7. Render to all their dues
Christ's saying about tribute to Caesar must underlie this
instruction (see Mark 12.17).

8-10. LAW AND LOVE

Mention of debt-paying reminds Paul that there is one debt never finally to be discharged—the debt of love to one's neighbour. To pay this debt is to fulfil the law. Take any of the commandments (he says) which bear on our behaviour towards our neighbour: they are all fulfilled in the single commandment of love. Why? Because LOVE WORKETH NO ILL TO HIS NEIGHBOUR; that is, the man who loves his neighbour—who really cares for him—will never dream of injuring him by taking his wife, his property or his life. In that sense, LOVE IS THE FULFILMENT OF THE LAW. Once again in Paul's sentences we catch echoes of him who summed up man's whole duty in the twin command of love to God and love to man (cf. Mark 12.29ff., Luke 10.26-28).

11-14. ETHICS OF REVEILLE

Paul rounds off this section with a call to his readers as children of the dawn to be 'up and doing' and to gird on the armour of light.

Christians resemble people living in some Alpine valley: high overhead, the mountains wear the gold of morning; and though darkness still lingers below, the first shafts of morning have illumined their faces (cf. Luke 1.78, 'The day-spring from on high hath visited us'). It is high time not only to be astir but to be putting on garments suitable to the new day.

The new day for Paul is of course the day of Christ's 'royal' coming (the *parousia*) when 'he who is our life shall appear' (Col. 3.4). We know that earlier in his career (when he wrote the Thessalonian letters) he believed that coming to be very near. If later (as in Romans and the prison letters) he dwells more on the present blessedness of believers and less on the imminence of the *parousia*, it still shines for him like a brilliant star in his spiritual sky. Nineteen hundred years have passed since Paul wrote, and Christ's Second Advent has not yet occurred. Yet the truth

for which the symbol of the Second Advent stands—that
God must complete his saving work begun in Christ and
that when the human race reaches its last frontier post, it
will come face to face not with nothingness but with God in
Christ—is integral to any true Christian theology. Moreover, we must remember that God stands above as well as
at the end of history; and since the eternal world is ever
breaking into this one, the Christian warrior must constantly
be alert to the challenge of Paul's *reveille*. On him is laid
the duty to strip off THE WORKS OF DARKNESS (the deeds of
the flesh) and to put on the ARMOUR of the new day. This
may be summarily described as putting ON THE LORD JESUS
CHRIST, i.e., entering ever more truly into the realization of
our membership in Christ, especially by clothing ourselves
in the moral habits of him who is the Captain of our
salvation.

Not in revelling and drunkenness, not in chambering and wantonness

Historic words. This verse and the following were those
which met Augustine's eyes when, sorrowing over his sins,
he heard a voice from some near-by house chanting *Tolle,
lege* ('Take and read'). He obeyed, found these words in
Romans—and was converted.

14. Put ye on the Lord Jesus Christ

For Paul, the entire Christian life can be described as a
constant putting off and a putting on. It begins with baptism
(Gal. 3.27). But since 'the perseverance of the saints consists in ever new beginnings', what happened in baptism
must ever take place anew.

XIV

PARAPHRASE

'*A word about weak brethren. I want you to welcome them. You strong Christians feel you may eat anything, as you believe no day is holier than another. But you must be tolerant towards the scruples of weak brethren who boggle at meat and observe special days. Let each respect the sincere conviction of the other, remembering that we all belong to Christ. An end to judging! We must all appear before the Supreme Judge!*

Granted, nothing is really unclean, but thinking may make it seem so. Let love be your law, and never count your food more important than Christ did his life. Pursue peace with all men, and think it better to abstain than cause offence. The man who hesitates and then eats does wrong, because he acts against his conscience.'

1-12. CHRISTIAN TOLERATION

This chapter forms an appendix to Paul's exposition of the Christian ethic. Having declared love to be the key to Christian behaviour, he now shows how it works in actual practice.

Two groups of Christian people, whom he calls 'the strong' and 'the weak', are addressed. Was Paul moved to write this chapter because he had heard of actual controversy between these two groups in the Church at Rome? And if so, who is the man WEAK IN FAITH—i.e. immaturely Christian? If some special situation concerns him, the man may have been any Christian, Jew or Gentile, worried about eating meat which he believed spiritually tainted because it had been consecrated to pagan idols before reaching the butchers' shops (cf. I Cor. 8-10). Alternatively, he was a

Jewish Christian who, like the Essenes, had serious scruples
about meat-eating and holy days (cf. Gal. 4.10f. and Col.
2.16f.). But perhaps Paul is talking quite generally, without
any special knowledge of Rome. In that case, he chooses
meat-eating and the observance of special days as illustra-
tions of the kind of difficulty which might put a strain on
Christian love in any church. When such friction arises
between 'scrupulists' and 'libertarians', the rule (he says)
should be Christian toleration on both sides. While indirectly pointing out the errors of the weak, he lays the
obligations squarely on the strong. 'No cold-shouldering
or criticizing of your weak brethren, please', he counsels
the strong. 'Some of you strong Christians believe you
may eat anything, and that no one day is holier than another.
Yes, but your fellowship contains also vegetarians and sab-
batarians with delicate scruples about these things. Well,
use these differences of opinion as opportunities for Christian toleration. We are all alike members of the Saviour's
family, and each should respect the sincere conviction of
the other, looking to Christ whose dying and rising has
made him Lord of all. An end to all judging! Those liable
themselves to judgment should not judge.'

The lesson in Christian toleration which Paul reads both
groups is capable of endless application to our contemporary
Christian problems.

1. Yet not to doubtful disputations
'Not for disputes over opinions' (RSV) is a better and
clearer translation.

4 Who art thou that judgest the servant of another?
The other is Christ. And Christ's JUDGE NOT (Matt. 7.1)
seems to underlie Paul's question.

Yea, he shall be made to stand
i.e. 'No gloomy views about your brother's chances of

being saved! His salvation is not in your hands but his Saviour's, and save him Christ can.'

6. In modern parlance: 'The meat-eater who says grace over his steak gives God glory; but so also does the vegetarian who asks a blessing on his salad.'

7f. None of us liveth to himself

The point is not our mutual interdependence; it is that we belong to Christ only. And that holds for death as well as life.

9. Through Christ's Resurrection his Lordship over the realm of death is established, so that not even in that dark world do those who are his cease to belong to him.

10f. Again an echo of Christ's JUDGE NOT. In face of our common responsibility to the Supreme Judge, how dare we judge each other? (Cf. II Cor. 5.10.) To illustrate the fact of universal judgment, Paul cites Isa. 45.23.

13-21. CHRISTIAN CONSIDERATENESS

Paul now addresses the strong Christians. He describes the influences which their conduct in matters morally indifferent may have on less enlightened people. The rule should be considerateness for the weaker brother. The 'fads' and 'peculiarities' of the weak brother to-day may be quite different, but the apostle's teaching retains its relevance—it is wisely and timelessly Christian.

13-18. In words which recall our Lord's teaching about 'stumbling-blocks' (*skandala:* temptations to sin—see Mark 9.42, Matt. 18.7 and Luke 17.1f.). Paul warns them not to be the occasion of their brother's falling. To be sure, nothing is, in its own nature, unclean (cf. Mark 7.14-23); yet to an over-scrupulous person something not in itself unclean may appear so, subjectively, and that person's conscience deserves our respect. For example, a strong brother whose meat-eating shocks his weak fellow-Christian, sins against the law of love. ' Christ died to save this man from his sins ', Paul says to the strong Christian, ' and will you not, for his sake, give up eating some favourite dish? You must not let your Christian freedom get itself a bad name. The meaning of membership in the Kingdom of God—the new order which has come with Christ's coming—is not that we can eat and drink what we like—these are quite minor matters—but that we can live, by the Spirit's power, the new radiant life of men accepted by God and filled with his peace. A man who SERVES CHRIST thus—i.e. shows consideration for his weak brother—pleases God and wins even the world's approval.'

19-21. Remembering how our act may affect the other man's Christian growth, we should always aim at mutual upbuilding. ' All things are clean '—agreed! Paul readily accepts the strong Christian's principle; yet he insists that it is wrong when the exercise of his Christian freedom wounds his brother's conscience. There is a Christian duty of self-restraint. In cases like these the honourable (*kalon*) course is to refuse to do anything which might hurt him.

22f. The strong Christian should therefore keep his FAITH —his assurance of the Spirit's guidance—a matter between himself and God, not flaunting it in his weak brother's face, but counting himself fortunate not to have a prickly conscience. For the weak brother to eat something about which he feels grave hesitations is to court moral disaster. Since FAITH—sincere Christian conviction—does not inform his action, it is bad.

15. For whom Christ died

Those who meet at the foot of the Cross find that

they are spiritual blood brothers and must act as such—

> *Blood brothers we became there*
> *And gentlemen each one.*

16. Your good

What is good to you, your Christian freedom, 'your rights' (Moffatt).

20. Overthrow not for meat's sake the work of God

Christian history, alas, shows numerous examples of people utterly earnest about non-essentials, who have felt at liberty to break the unity of the Church for the sake of their particular fetish.

23. Whatsoever is not of faith is sin

A text often misunderstood and misused. It does not mean that the acts of all non-Christians are sins. Chrysostom understood it: 'When a person,' he writes, 'does not feel sure, nor believe that a thing is clean, how can he do else than sin? Now all these things have been spoken by Paul of the object in hand, not of everything.'

XV

' *Let the strong bear with the weak. Christ did not please himself, no more should we. Since he has received you both, you should receive each other. Did he not come as God's servant to break down the barrier between Jew and Gentile, that both together might glorify God?*

My dear readers, I know you are good and knowledgeable people. My frankness in this letter springs from my zeal as apostle to the Gentiles. I feel that I am offering up the Gentile Church to God like a priest at the altar. What a mighty work God has enabled me to do in preaching the Gospel from Jerusalem to Illyricum! For it has been a point of honour with me always to choose regions which have never heard of Christ.

Now, my work here done, I hope to go to Spain, halting at Rome en route. *At the moment, however, I am off to Jerusalem with a contribution from the Gentile churches for the poor saints there. Pray for me as I go among the Jewish unbelievers that my gift may be graciously received and I may be free to visit you. The God of peace be with you.*'

1-6. Paul concludes his counsels to WEAK and STRONG. The ' strong ' (with whom, by his WE, Paul ranks himself) should bear with the INFIRMITIES—the qualms and ' querulosities '—of the ' weak ', and each should seek his neighbour's good. As in Phil. 2.4f., Paul carries this obligation back to Christ, the supreme Exemplar, whose selfless conduct he describes in a verse from Psalm 69. (In passing, he justifies this appeal to the scriptures. They are there for us to learn from them both patience and comfort that we in our turn may hold fast our Christian hope.) May the God who inspires

such patience and comfort enable them to live in harmony
with each other, following Christ's example (*kata Christon*),
that strong and weak together may unite in the worship of
THE GOD AND FATHER OF OUR LORD JESUS CHRIST.

7-13. These verses are difficult. We may try to paraphrase
Paul's thought thus: ' Welcome each other, then, as Christ,
who is your Example, has received both groups among you
into his fellowship. Surely you can forget your divisions
and receive each other, remembering how much greater was
the racial division he had to overcome. When the Saviour
was born a Jew (lit. " a servant of circumcision "), he had not
only to fulfil God's ancient promises of salvation to his own
People, but also to bring God's mercy to the outcast Gentiles.
By his selfless service he succeeded so that now, in one
family, the Gentiles can worship along with God's People,
as the scriptures predicted. From Jesse's root God has
provided the Saviour, and a new hope has come not to Israel
only but to the Gentile world too: " in him shall the Gentiles
hope." May the God of hope give you that peace and joy
which are the happy fruits of true faith that, enabled by the
Spirit, your whole life may be radiant with hope.'

'Radiant with hope.' In Romans, HOPE (the modern
Cinderella in Paul's triad of Christian graces) comes into her
own. WE REJOICE IN HOPE OF THE GLORY OF GOD: TRIBULA-
TION WORKETH PATIENCE, AND PATIENCE, CHARACTER, AND
CHARACTER, HOPE—A HOPE THAT DOES NOT PUT US TO
SHAME—so he writes in chapter 5. Romans 8, where we
read that WE WERE SAVED IN HOPE, is one long diapason on
the hope which is ours in Christ, culminating in Paul's great
'persuasion' that nothing in this world or out of it can
separate us from the love of God. And now, near the end,
he prays that believers may abound in that hope. Paul a
gloomy apostle? Never! Realist? Yes—see Romans
1.16–3.20. But for all his ' full look at the worst ', no Christian has surpassed Paul's invincible certitude that God is

working out a good purpose for us and for all men and will
surely bring it to a blessed conclusion.

1. Bear

means 'shoulder the burden of'. The verb *bastazein* is
used in the Gospels of cross-bearing: Luke 14.27 and John
19.17.

3. Ps. 69.9. Paul interprets the verse as a confession of
Christ who has taken on himself the insults meant for God.

9-12. A string of quotations from the Old Testament—Ps.
18.49, Deut. 32.43, Ps. 117.1 and Isa. 11.10—all attesting
the universality of salvation, as another catena in 3.10-18
had attested the universality of sin.

CONCLUSION OF THE EPISTLE
15.14–16.27

14-21. PAUL AND HIS READERS

Paul's exposition of the Christian faith and the Christian
way is over. It remains to say a few words to his readers,
to sketch his travel-plans, and to send greetings.

Observe his tact and modesty. 'I know very well,' he
says, 'that you are good and knowledgeable people. All
my letter aims to do is to remind you of a few points you may
have forgotten.' Yet these 'few points' add up to one of
the greatest Christian letters ever written.

If he has been rather forthright (he says) it is because he
is conscious of a divine commission. To describe his work,
he employs a sacerdotal metaphor. He calls himself a
leitourgos ('a sacred minister') performing a priestly function (*hierourgounta*) for the gospel. Before the altar, so to
say, he stands as the priest of the gospel, and the offering
he makes is nothing less than the Gentile Church, his hope
being that, consecrated as it is by the Holy Spirit, it may

prove acceptable to God. IN CHRIST—and in him only—he
' has reason to be proud of his work for God '. His sole
theme must be what Christ has achieved through him for
the conversion of the Gentiles, and this apostolic labour has
been marked by all the supernatural signs of the new order
—effective preaching and miraculous happenings—which
proclaim the presence and power of the Holy Spirit.

He describes the limits of his labours—FROM JERUSALEM,
AND ROUND ABOUT EVEN UNTO ILLYRICUM—' from Jerusalem
to Jugoslavia, tracing a wide circle round ', we might say.
Illyricum was the Roman province, lying north of Macedonia
and looking across the Adriatic to Italy. Does Paul mean
that he has actually laboured there? Acts says nothing
about it, and perhaps all he means is that in his westward
Macedonian mission he has reached its frontiers. Always
his ambition has been to plant the Cross in some *terra nova*,
and not to reap an evangelic harvest where some other has
sowed already. And such procedure accords with what was
written of the Lord's Servant (Isa. 52.15).

19. Signs and wonders

Sēmeia and *terata*. The latter word stresses the marvel-
lous nature of the events, the former their divine significance.

22-23. PAUL'S PLANS

For years Paul has been cherishing the dream of taking
the gospel westwards to Rome the Imperial City and there-
after to Spain. Now, with his work in Asia and Greece
done, the dream looks like coming true. But, first, he must
journey in the opposite direction—to Jerusalem. For,
besides the Roman visit, he has, for long, been setting in
train another project (of which we hear first in Galatians
and then in the Corinthian Epistles), the raising of a relief
fund for the poor saints of the mother church. The poverty
of the Jerusalem Christians was real enough, and Paul hoped
his collection would alleviate it. But he hoped also, as we

may see here, that his gift of monetary aid would be an *eirēnikon*—a gesture of goodwill from himself to his fellow-countrymen who still regarded him with hatred. And if the Jerusalem Christians received his gift in the spirit in which it was offered, there might follow a relaxing of the tension between the conservative Jewish-Christian wing of the Church and the advanced missionary one represented by St. Paul.

To this relief-fund Paul's churches in Macedonia and Achaia had readily agreed to contribute. Yet while stressing their readiness, he insists that they are only discharging a just debt. For if the Gentiles have shared in the Jews' spiritual 'good things' (the gospel), it is but fair that they should share with them their material blessings.

But clouds hang over Jerusalem, and Paul is not sure that they are 'big with blessing'. His unbelieving fellow-Jews mean him no good, and even the Jewish Christians have not shed all suspicion of the ex-persecutor. So he asks the prayers of the Roman Christians for himself that his Jerusalem mission may succeed. (We cannot miss the parallel between Paul and his Lord in Gethsemane. Like Christ, Paul is urging his friends to watch with him. As Christ knows that a cross awaits him, so Paul is aware that his life is in jeopardy. In such a crisis the need for the sympathy of friends is acutely felt. Therefore he begs his readers by the most potent constraints he can put on them— by the Lord whom they worship and by the love which the Spirit creates—that they will join him in 'an almost convulsive energy of supplication'.) Should all go well, he will come to Rome with Christ's blessing and may hope there, after a little rest, to be sped forward by the Roman Christians on his Spanish mission.

Paul's fears were not unfounded. Luke tells us what happened (Acts 21.27ff.). Jewish hatred at Jerusalem so far succeeded that only Roman intervention saved his life. Reach Rome he did, eventually, but as a prisoner. Whether he ever set foot in Spain remains an unsolved mystery. 'He reached the limit of the west', says Clement of Rome writing a generation later; but whether the 'limit' denotes Gibraltar or only Rome, we cannot say.

24. To be brought on my way *(propemphthēnai)*

The Greek verb means practically to 'accredit a delegate', and possibly hints that Paul would like the Roman Church to take moral—and perhaps financial—responsibility for his Spanish mission.

28. Sealed to them this fruit

The FRUIT is the collection. The Greek verb *sphragizomai* translated 'seal' is a common commercial term in the papyri. Here it apparently means 'deliver safely'.

XVI

NOTE ON ROMANS 16

Some scholars believe that Romans 16 is not an integral part of Romans, but a separate letter to Ephesus in commendation of Phoebe. Here are the main points in their case:

1. Paul can hardly have known so many people in Rome as the numerous greetings imply.
2. Aquila and Priscilla, when we last hear of them (I Cor. 16.19. Cf. II Tim. 4.19), are in Ephesus.
3. The phrase APAENETUS . . . THE FIRSTFRUITS OF ASIA UNTO CHRIST suits Ephesus better than Rome.
4. The sharp warning of 16.17-20 consists ill with the conciliatory tone of the rest of Romans, but would be in place in a letter to Ephesus. Cf. Acts 20.29f.

The case, if strong, is not unanswerable.

Point (1) is effectively answered by the fact that Paul did not usually single out individuals for special greetings in a church he knew well (e.g. the churches at Corinth or Philippi). Significantly, he does include such greeting to the church at Colossae which he did not know personally.

Point (2) is weakened by the consideration that Aquila and Priscilla, who came originally from Rome, may very well have gone back there when the Emperor's decree against the Jews was relaxed. In Nero's reign Rome had many Jews.

If points (3) and (4) remain, we may set on the Roman side three considerations:

1. It is hard to believe that Romans 16 is a complete letter.
2. Rom. 16.16, ALL THE CHURCHES OF CHRIST SALUTE YOU,

suits Rome much better than Ephesus. At the time Paul was in close touch with representatives of the churches of Galatia, Asia, Macedonia and Achaia over the business of the relief-fund. What more natural than that they should back his appeal to the church in Rome?

3. Many of the persons named in the greetings can be connected in one way or another with Rome (see the notes in the commentary).

Clearly, the Ephesian theory falls far short of proof. In a case of this kind it is wise to prefer tradition to speculation.

PARAPHRASE

' *Allow me to introduce Phoebe, the deaconess of the Church at Cenchreae. Give her the Christian welcome she so well deserves.*

I send my best wishes to Prisca and Aquila, Epaenetus and all Christian friends in Rome.

(P.S. Beware of mischief-makers who may come among you and make trouble. Be wise and good. May Christ's grace be with you.)

Timothy, Lucius and the other friends in Corinth send their kind regards. (And so do I, Tertius, the scribe.)

I commend you all to God.
                                    PAUL.'

The chapter falls into five parts: (1) Commendation of Phoebe; (2) Greetings to Paul's friends in Rome; (3) Warning against false teachers; (4) Greetings from Paul's companions; and (5) the Doxology.

1-2. RECOMMENDATION OF PHOEBE

If PHOEBE took Paul's letter from Corinth to Rome, as seems likely, she carried under her robe, as Renan observed with pardonable hyperbole, the entire future of Christian theology. Paul styles her A SERVANT (lit. ' deacon ') OF THE CHURCH THAT IS AT CENCHREAE. Was she ' a deaconess '? ' Deaconesses ' figure in Pliny's correspondence with Trajan

some fifty years after this, and Paul speaks in Phil. 1.1 of
'bishops and deacons'. Where there are deacons, there
may well be deaconesses; but how far the office (if there
was one) had developed by, say, A.D. 57, we do not know.
Perhaps Phoebe was set apart by the church in Cenchreae
to care for the poor and the sick. She had been the 'helper'
(*prostatis*: lit. 'patroness') of many, including Paul himself
(Did she 'lodge' him or look after him when sick?), and the
apostle bespeaks for her a worthy Christian welcome in
Rome.

3-16. GREETINGS TO ROME

Why so many greetings? We may may surmise that,
realizing how important the Roman church's help would be
for his work in the West, he was anxious to recall as many
'contacts' in the capital as he could. Some of the twenty-
six people named he must have known personally; about
others he may merely have heard from Aquila, Priscilla and
others. To each name, as he dictates it, he adds a brief
phrase of compliment or a detail linking the person with
himself.

3-5. Pride of place goes to PRISCA ('Priscilla' is the diminu-
tive) and AQUILA—note the order: in four out of six NT
references to the couple, the lady's name comes first: she
was obviously the more important person, and, even if she
did not write the Epistle to the Hebrews (as some scholars
have guessed), stands high in the New Testament's list of
noted women. From this and the other NT references (Acts
18.2, 18, 26, I Cor. 16.19 and II Tim. 4.19) we gather something of their story. Expelled from Rome following the
Emperor Claudius's decree against the Jews in A.D. 49, they
had encountered Paul in Corinth. Thence they had
travelled with him to Ephesus, where they still stayed when
he wrote I Cor. 16.19. Probably it was in Ephesus, during
the trouble there, that they had 'risked their necks' for the

apostle. Since Claudius died in 54, not improbably the couple went back to Rome (where there were many Jews in Nero's time) and opened their house for worship there, as they had done in Ephesus.

5-16. The number of people in Rome known to him should not surprise us unduly. Commerce in the Roman Empire was brisk, and business must have taken many of Paul's acquaintances to the capital. Greek, Latin and Jewish names lie cheek by jowl with each other in the list of ' salutes'. Eight of the twenty-six seem to be women, and many of them (e.g. Ampliatus, Phlegon and Persis) have names commonly borne by slaves: an indication of the social stratum from which the early Church recruited many of its members (cf. I Cor. 1.26). Some are Paul's fellow countrymen, i.e. Jewish Christians (Andronicus, Junias and Herodion), for such must be the force of KINSMEN here. The others are Romans and Greeks with at least one Asiatic.

The Asiatic is EPAENETUS. Clearly Paul was proud of him as ' the first convert in Asia for Christ'. After MARY (who may have been either a Jew or a Gentile) come two Jews, ANDRONICUS AND JUNIAS, of whom we learn three things. First, they had been Christians before Paul and therefore conceivably members of the mother church in Jerusalem. Second, they were APOSTLES, i.e. ' accredited evangelists' of high standing (*episēmoi*) (the word ' apostle' being used here not in its narrower but in its wider sense). And, third, on some notable occasion they had shared Paul's imprisonment. AMPLIATUS, the next to be named, may be the man whose tomb in Rome, ' decorated with paintings in a very early style, bears the one word "Ampliati" in fine uncial lettering of the first or early second century.'[1] Of the names which follow—URBANUS, STACHYS, APELLES, HERODION (a Jew whose name suggests the Herod family), TRYPHAENA AND TRYPHOSA (' Dainty' and ' Delicate'—per-

[1] Dodd, *Romans, ad loc.*

haps twin sisters) and PERSIS (' that hard-working Christian ')
—we know nothing beyond what Paul tells us. RUFUS,
however, may well be the man mentioned in Mark 15.21,
the brother of Alexander. If so, his father was Simon of
Cyrene who carried Christ's cross. Paul tells us two things
about him. First, his mother had ' mothered ' Paul at some
time, and, second, the son himself was ELECT IN THE LORD,
in other words, ' a choice Christian '. (What Christian ante-
cedents to possess! A father who had carried the Saviour's
cross, and a mother who had ' mothered ' his greatest
apostle! This red-haired man—if we may press the meaning of his name—had ' something to boast about in the
Lord '.)

The rest—ASYNCRITUS, PHLEGON, HERMES, PATROBAS,
HERMAS (not the author of *The Shepherd of Hermas*),
PHILOLOGUS, JULIA, NEREUS AND HIS SISTER, and OLYMPAS
—are mere names to us. But we do well to note the two
groups named THE HOUSEHOLD OF ARISTOBULUS and THE
HOUSEHOLD OF NARCISSUS. The first group may have been
former slaves of a grandson of Herod the Great bearing the
name Aristobolus who lived and died as a private person in
Rome, enjoying the favour of the Emperor Claudius.
Similarly we may guess that ' the people of Narcissus ' were
former slaves of one Narcissus, a freedman of the Imperial
House, who exercised great influence under Claudius and
was put to death soon after Nero became emperor. On
Narcissus's death his slaves would naturally pass, with his
other property, into the Emperor's possession.

16. Salute one another with a holy kiss

We may conjecture that Paul meant them to do this when
they met to hold the Lord's Supper and Paul's letter would
be read aloud. From Justin Martyr we know that the holy
kiss formed part of the liturgy in Rome about 150, and
the Greek Orthodox Church preserves the custom at the
Eucharist to this day.

17-20. WARNING AGAINST FALSE TEACHERS

Quite abruptly, between Paul's greetings and those of his companions, comes a sharp warning against false teachers (cf. Gal. 6.11-16 and Phil. 3.18-19). These people, Paul says, create divisions and troubles, actuated as they are, not by devotion to Christ but by their own self-interest (this is what THEY SERVE THEIR OWN BELLY means), and the simple-minded are easily beguiled by their flattering tongues.

Has Paul in his mind his old enemies, the Judaisers (as in Galatians and Philippians), or are these men antinomian reactionaries who defended their immoral ways in the name of Christian freedom? We do not know. What seems clear is that they had not yet begun work in Rome. Still, the danger is real, and Paul bids his readers 'give them a wide berth'. Confident of their Christian obedience, he counsels them (perhaps echoing the Lord's saying in Matt. 10.16) to be 'experts in good and innocents in evil'. Such false teachers are tools of the devil, but THE GOD OF PEACE may be trusted to defeat all their stratagems (cf. the primeval promise in Gen. 3.15).

21-24. GREETINGS FROM PAUL'S COMPANIONS

Now it is the turn of Paul's eight friends in Corinth to send greetings. The first is TIMOTHY, Paul's staunch co-adjutor in the mission-field. LUCIUS (cf. Acts 13.1), JASON (cf. Acts 17.5-9) and SOSIPATER (perhaps the same man as in Acts 20.4) follow, all Jews. At this point, TERTIUS, the amanuensis who has penned the whole letter, scribbles in his own greetings—perhaps he had some friends in Rome—like some mason in the corner of the building he has made. Next comes GAIUS, MY HOST AND OF THE WHOLE CHURCH. He is surely the same as in I Cor. 1.14. We take Paul to mean that he was staying with Gaius, and that Gaius kept 'open house' for travelling Christians generally. He must have had a bigger house than most as well as more money.

The list ends with ERASTUS, the city-treasurer of Corinth and another Christian named QUARTUS.

25-27. THE DOXOLOGY

The Doxology was probably no original part of Paul's letter. Though the separate ideas in it are Pauline, it reads like mosaic work, and was possibly composed by another hand than Paul's. Some MSS. put it here, others at the end of chapter 14, and P46 (the Chester Beatty MS.) has it at the end of 15. Perhaps some 'Paulinist' strung it together to form an impressive liturgical ending for the reading of Paul's letter in church.

According to my gospel

reminds us of Rom. 2.16. It must mean the one apostolic gospel presented with Paul's own emphases on the absolute freeness of salvation and the absolute universality of the gospel. PREACHING is in Greek *kērygma*, a word practically equivalent to 'gospel'. Pauline too is the next idea of the secret purpose of God long veiled and now disclosed in Christ.

According to the commandment of the eternal God

recalls the style of the Pastoral Epistles, as OBEDIENCE TO THE FAITH takes us back to 1.5. The words TO WHOM in the last verse should probably be omitted.

> *To God all-wise be glory*
> *Who strength hath given to men*
> *By making known his secret*
> *Long hid from human ken.*
>
> *Prophetic voices told it*
> *To ears that closed again,*
> *But now to faithful Pagans*
> *He makes the mystery plain.*[1]

[1] J. W. C. Wand, *The New Testament Letters*, 103.